GIVE THANKS TO THE LORD

Nihil Obstat:
The Reverend John Roos, J.C.D.
Censor Librorum

Imprimatur:
The Most Reverend Howard J. Hubbard, D.D.
Bishop of Albany
November 23, 1993

GIVE THANKS TO THE LORD

Passing on the Faith
Through
Mealtime Prayer and Catholic Devotion

ROBERT G. DESMOND

Foreword by
HOWARD J. HUBBARD, BISHOP OF ALBANY

KERYGMATIC PUBLICATIONS
Proclaiming the Lord and His Church

Kerygmatic Publications
Proclaiming the Lord and His Church
204 Pleasant Vale Road
Tivoli, NY 12583-5205

Produced by
Peter E. Randall Publisher, Portsmouth, New Hampshire 03802

Dedicated
to
The Greater Glory
of
Our Lord and Savior

JESUS CHRIST

Many people who admit little likelihood of Divine communication with ordinary human beings quite readily blame the devil for all sorts of temptations and personal failings. The words of Scripture that say "Your opponent the devil is prowling around like a roaring lion looking for [someone] to devour" (1 Pet 5:8) and the principalities and powers of Ephesians 6:12 seem to hold more importance than the realization that God loves each of us individually and totally. I believe it is just as likely that God and His angels and saints communicate with us in the form of thoughts and inspirations intended to lead us closer to our Creator. It was just such a thought during a period of prayer that led to the dedication of this work. While considering a dedication to our Blessed Lady and meditating on her participation in God's plan of salvation this thought came to mind: "Dedicate it to the glory of my Son. My only purpose is to lead you to Him."

FOREWORD

As Robert Desmond notes in his Preface to this book, "If children are to learn to pray, I believe it is essential for them to have the opportunity to participate in family prayer from an early age." That comment expresses the essence of *Give Thanks to the Lord: Passing on the Faith Through Mealtime Prayer and Catholic Devotion.* Centered in the gathering of a family meal, the beautiful prayer of grace at mealtime is the core of the reflections and the suggestions, rooted in Scripture, in tradition, in devotional prayer, and in communal praise and thanksgiving which the author shares with his readers.

This book uses the framework of the Church year to provide suggestions for appropriate themes and prayers for the given seasons and feasts, unified by the central prayer at mealtime. Desmond draws upon Biblical and historical sources of prayer for a better understanding of its past and present forms. He gives prominent attention to devotion to Mary and especially to the Rosary, prayed with Scriptural reflection on its Mysteries.

Throughout the work, the author provides numerous references to books and other resource materials that will assist the family in strengthening its prayer life and in growing in understanding of the effects of prayer upon one's relationship with God, with one another, and with the larger community. Desmond draws upon his own family prayer experience to illustrate such efforts toward growth in the prayer life of the family and the vitalizing effects that such growth can set in motion.

The consistent tone of Robert Desmond's book is one of hope and of rejoicing in its core theme of mealtime prayer and Catholic devotion. The reflections and the suggestions contained in his work support its very purpose. In a time in which so many families suffer such painful divisions and brokenness, Desmond offers the alternative of a family gathering at a meal and seeking together to be healed, strengthened, and enabled by God, author of all hospitality and community, and reaching out to share these experiences with others.

Most Rev. Howard J. Hubbard
Bishop of Albany
November 1, 1992

TABLE OF CONTENTS

IN GRATEFUL APPRECIATION

As I near completion of this work and reflect back on a lifetime of preparation, I am reminded of the words of John Donne: "No man is an island."

The seed for this book was planted more than thirty years ago while I was serving in the U.S. Army. During a discussion of prayer and the family Rosary, a friend mentioned that his parents used to vary their family prayer according to the liturgical seasons and would make appropriate commemorations at mealtime. We have followed his family's example, making many adaptations over the years. We have found the mealtime gathering of the family provides a perfect opportunity for shared faith experiences.

The preparation for this work, however, can be traced back even further and I must acknowledge several debts from my adolescent years.

My mother passed on to her eternal reward when I was eleven years old and my sister only six. My father, with much difficulty and the help of relatives and friends, managed to keep the three of us together as a family. Although he did not share our Catholic Faith, he always made sure that we got to Sunday Mass. In this regard we were blessed by the help and generosity of many people; most notably the Luther B. Martin family who regularly transported us to the next town for Sunday Mass.

As Roman Catholics living in the small New England town, of East Hartland, Connecticut, we were in the minority. On many occasions friends and school-mates (in those pre-ecumenical times) were more than willing to remind us of that fact and show us the "error of our ways," but, even here, the Lord was already at work in my life. Our (mostly) friendly exchanges and discussions only served to ignite and fan a flame of interest which has not died to this day.

I am also deeply indebted to Father Dominic Avampato, whose first parish assignment as a young priest was to St. Theresa's, the parish of my youth in Granby, Connecticut. It was Father Dom who first introduced me to the writings and teachings of St. Louis-Marie Grignion De Montfort and who unquestionably exerted the most positive influence in my early spiritual development.

From the beginning this effort has been a family affair in both the living and the writing of the experience. May God grant His special blessing to John and BethAnn for their word for word comparison of original and typed manuscripts; to David and John for their extra efforts in the yard and garden, thereby allowing me more time for writing; and especially to Theresa for her heroic effort in typing and retyping the entire manuscript. And most especially I am indebted to my devoted wife Eva who joined me in our first family Rosary on our wedding day. She has been a constant and faithful helpmate whose love and unselfish devotion to family has probably exerted a greater positive influence on our children than all their other religious education experiences combined.

My thanks to the many friends who read and commented on all or part of the manuscript. I am particularly grateful to Father Randal Gillette, C.P. for his critique, suggestions and words of encouragement.

Finally, as I reflect on all the assistance I have received I must make one other acknowledgement: Throughout the entire time of writing I have attempted to remain open to the inspiration of the Holy Spirit and I must confess that anything good in this work is due to the grace of God, while anything lacking is surely due to my own inability to be totally open and in tune with the will of God. I long ago lost count of the number of times I sat with a blank mind, unable to find the proper words, only to find new inspiration as I turned my thoughts and prayers to the Lord. I was constantly reminded of the truth of the words of our Lord as recorded in verse 5 of the 15th chapter of John's Gospel, "I am the vine, you are the branches. Whoever remains in me and I in him will bear much fruit, because without me you can do nothing."

PREFACE

If children are to learn to pray, I believe it is essential for them to have the opportunity to participate in family prayer from an early age. If they are to develop a mature faith, a stable and genuine faith-filled environment must be provided during their formative years. Many studies have shown that parents are the most important people in developing a child's spiritual awareness, yet we find many parents who believe themselves incapable of fostering a genuine spirituality in the home, or who are disinterested in doing so.

Our modern, fast paced society attracts family members in many and varied directions. Family life and traditional Christian values are under constant attack on all fronts. The media present values that continually emphasize consumerism and self-indulgence, and we face a secular world that is increasingly hostile to the Word of God. Our young people are further driven by peer pressure to measure up to these worldly standards. Parents who desire a moral and spiritual upbringing for their children often find themselves unable to compete with the cultural pressures arrayed against them. We need to find new and varied approaches to bring the faith alive within our families.

While I have certainly experienced my share of mistakes, my wife and I have also been blessed with much success in our efforts to develop a sense of family spirituality. In this book I have attempted to share some of our experiences and present our approach to family mealtime prayer and traditional Catholic devotions as an aid to spiritual development. It is our hope and prayer that our thoughts and suggestions may help other families to develop closer bonds between themselves and their loving Father in Heaven.

How to use this book

This book is meant to be more than just a book to read once and put away. It is meant to provide background information for supplemental religious education in the home. It is intended to encourage family prayer and it is offered as an aid to Christian meditation.

It should first be read through for familiarization though even here there is room for variety. The book may be approached as a collection of short stories. If you find a chapter that does not particularly appeal to you, simply pass over it and go on to the next. Or if you see something in the table of contents that draws your interest, read it first and then go back to the others.

An aid to family prayer

Once you have become familiar with the contents, you are ready to expand the use of the book as mentioned above. As an aid to family prayer you can pick and choose those suggestions which you find appropriate for your family. Also, as you read of our experiences you may be inspired to develop family prayer practices of your own.

In each chapter, I have provided not only specific background on a particular devotion, but basic Christian teaching as well. Many of the traditional devotions lend themselves very easily to discussions of our faith, and it is these discussions which allow us to pass on the faith to our children. While additional reading may be helpful, I have attempted in each chapter to establish a theme for discussion and provide sufficient background information to give proper perspective to the place of the devotion in the mainstream of Christian life.

Mealtime prayer-learning experience

In our family, mealtime provided the most effective setting for supplemental religious education in the home. In what we call a mealtime prayer-learning experience we combine a periodic after-dinner discussion with a daily commemoration or addition to our grace before meals. The daily commemoration acts as a painless reinforcement of the after-dinner discussion. The discussion and commemoration center around a common monthly or seasonal theme. Most of the chapters in the book provide background and source material for the monthly or seasonal themes of the mealtime prayer-learning experiences. The concept and format of the mealtime prayer-learning experience will be more fully explained in Chapter III.

An aid to meditation

Many of the chapters can also be used as an aid to meditation. For many, meditation is an unfamiliar experience. To some it is an activity which is proper only in the monastery or convent, while others think meditation requires a degree of spiritual sophistication which they judge to be lacking in themselves.

Actually, Christian meditation is an uncomplicated spiritual exercise in which the benefits far outweigh the effort required.

To meditate is simply to think about and reflect upon the mysteries and truths of Christianity. The focus might be on an incident in the life of our Lord, or upon our own personal response to the Christian message. While there are no set or absolute rules to follow in meditation, a few simple steps may be helpful for the beginner. The suggested sequence is preparation, reflection and prayer; each step is simple and briefly explained below.

PREPARATION consists primarily of reading, although an inspiring homily can also provide a preparation for meditation. The choice for preparation might be as short as a single Scriptural verse or a much longer selection of spiritual reading. If the selected readings are long, the preparation can take place at a different time. The Ignation method of meditation, for example, suggests a remote preparation the night before, with the actual prayer and meditation time on the following morning.

REFLECTION is simply thinking about the subject of the meditation. Often, as we meditate, God will inspire our thoughts and we experience a special closeness to Him.

PRAYER in meditation is nothing more than talking to God in our own words which we may address to the Father, the Son or the Holy Spirit. We simply pour out our innermost thoughts, as we would to a close personal friend. We may tell Him our troubles or we may offer consolation for His sufferings. Perhaps, we'll recognize our own shortcomings and ask His help in living a better life. Whatever form our prayer takes, it is our own personal meeting with the Lord and He is there with us. At some point in our prayer we may stop and listen to God speak in the depths of our inner being.

As our meditation time progresses, the structure becomes less important. We may drift back and forth between reflection and prayer or even to preparation as we read a few more lines. The distinctions between preparation, reflection and prayer tend to fade as we just spend time with the Lord in the company of His angels and saints whom we may also address from time to time.

A tremendous peace can come from this relationship with the Lord. It is recommended not only for our spiritual well being but for our mental and physical health as well. Many physicians who recognize the detrimental effects of stress and tension have recommended prayer and meditation as an antidote to the pressures of daily living.

Perhaps a few examples will help: Suppose you want to meditate on the Passion and suffering of our Lord. An extended preparation might consist of reading Chapter VI and the reflections associated with the Sorrowful Mysteries of the Rosary in Chapter XVII. After reading this material, go back and slowly re-read a section which describes a portion of the Passion, then think about the particular incident. Imagine what it would have been like to actually be there; imagine the sights, the sounds, and try to mentally place yourself in the scene. Think of what our Lord went through. Think of why. Think of His love for us and our all-too-often indifferent response to Him. Talk to Him, console Him and ask His help in living a better life. Then stop and listen to His response deep within your own heart and soul.

Perhaps you want to meditate on the indwelling of the Holy Spirit. You might first read Chapters IX and XVI and the third Glorious Mystery from Chapter XVII. Then concentrate on a particular gift of the Holy Spirit. Consider the meaning and purpose of that gift and your own response to it. Talk to the Lord, thank Him for that gift, ask Him to help you to be more responsive to it, ask Him to pour forth His Spirit upon you so that you may grow in His love and peace and joy.

After reading chapters XI and XIV which provide background on the sacramental presence of our Lord, you might spend some time before the Blessed Sacrament reflecting on your response to this gift. Or, if you want to meditate on our final destiny, you might first read Chapter XVIII. Chapter XVII provides fifteen separate suggestions for meditation in the discussions of the fifteen Mysteries of the Rosary.

These mediation suggestions can be used at random or sequentially through the year. A period of private meditation is an excellent preparation for a family discussion of the monthly devotion. Meditation can also be a family affair. One member could read the preparatory material and then those who feel so moved might share their thoughts and reflections aloud. Shared prayer can also be a part of this exercise. This family meditation can have a valuable unifying effect on the family and introduce the children to a higher form of prayer at an early age.

I

Praise the Lord

A brief introduction to prayer

Prayer can be defined as an elevation of the mind and heart to God; to adore Him, to praise Him, to make reparation to Him, to thank Him and to ask His blessings. We can also define prayer as speaking to God and then listening to Him speak in our hearts. There are many reasons to pray and many ways to pray but ultimately the goal is always the same—a closer relationship with God. We can pray in our own words or someone else's words; sometimes we find the best prayer uses no words at all. We can pray in church, we can pray at home, we can pray at work. In fact, as we shall soon see, Saint Paul tells us we should pray constantly *(cf. Eph 6:18; 1 Thes 5:17)*.

The primary theme of this book is the mealtime blessing and the introduction of a mealtime prayer-learning experience which focuses on traditional Catholic devotions. The total Christian prayer life is much broader than this. Before we begin our concentration on mealtime prayer let's first look at the subject of prayer in general so that we can appreciate this specific prayer experience from a fuller and more complete perspective.

Let us first consider our attitude of prayer and look at what Scripture says concerning prayer, to find answers to questions such as: What is prayer? Why should we pray? When should we pray? How should we pray?

We should begin with the realization that it is God who perfects our prayer, for without Him there is no prayer. That may seem obvious but it is worthwhile to reflect for a moment and realize it is possible to repeat the words of a prayer without really praying. If we do not at least in some way acknowledge the existence of God and recognize His presence, our words of prayer become no more than senseless babbling or, at best, the equivalent of a poetry recitation. And yet, with the realization of God's presence, even a poetry recitation can become a prayer, as we will see later.

We can say then, that prayer begins with an interior attitude of the heart and an acknowledgment of our dependence upon our Creator. We are created by God and as such are completely dependent upon Him for our existence. We have been given the remarkable gift of rational intelligence and have been created in such a way that we have the ability to recognize and know our Creator. In view of this gift of recognition, which we receive through gifts of reason and revelation, we are bound in justice to acknowledge our dependence upon our Creator and His dominion over us.

Even more remarkable than the gift of intelligence is the gift of free will, which grants us the ability to freely choose or reject that acknowledgment of dependence. Our Creator has given us the ultimate gift of freedom, so that we can accept or reject His love which He will not force upon us.

Having freely chosen in our hearts to acknowledge our dependence upon Him and His dominion over us, we have taken our first step into a prayerful relationship with our Creator. As we open ourselves to God, He will respond with His love, and that relationship will grow.

God is constantly calling us to yield to a deeper and closer relationship with Him. As we open ourselves to Him in prayer He responds with His grace and we are drawn to seek even more of His love. God calls us in many ways and sometimes when our prayers do not seem to be answered it is because He wants us to learn perseverance. We find this message in the Gospel parables of the corrupt judge *(cf. Lk 18:1-8)* or the midnight request for bread *(cf. Lk 11:5-8)*. Another example of perseverance in prayer has been given to us by Saint Monica, who is said to have prayed for the conversion of her son for twenty years. After years of living a notorious life of sin, her son repented and became the great Saint Augustine.

Saint Paul tells us much about prayer in his letters. In one way or another Paul speaks of prayer in almost every letter. We find a constantly recurring theme of Christian interdependence through prayer in Paul's letters. He tells his readers that he prays for them and thanks God for them *(cf. 2 Thes 1:11; 2 Tim 1:3; 1 Cor 1:4)* and he asks them to pray for him *(cf. 2 Thes 3:1-2; Phlm 1:22)*. Paul even calls his readers to take a real part in his ministry through their prayers *(cf. Rom 15:30-32; 2 Cor 1:11; Eph 6:18-20)*.

In his first letter to the Thessalonians Paul goes so far as to tell us to "Pray without ceasing" *(1 Thes 5:17)*. This would seem to exclude all other activity, and yet we know that Paul recognized the need for other activities as he further tells the Thessalonians to work with their own hands and that anyone unwilling to work shouldn't eat *(cf. 1 Thes 4:11; 2 Thes 3:10)*.

Is Paul's call to unceasing prayer to be taken figuratively rather than literally? I think not. What Paul is calling for is that inner conversion, that change in attitude in which one recognizes a total dependence on God and wills to live totally in that dependence. In this way each and every proper action of life becomes a prayer, as we realize that this action is what God has called us to at that moment.

Many people renew that dedication each day with a *morning offering* in which the coming day's activities are offered and consecrated to the greater glory of God.

Prayer then, is essentially an attitude of the inner being and requires no specific overt actions. We find, however, that this inner attitude will not be long sustained without some exterior manifestation and so we find that Paul also tells us to "pray at every opportunity" *(Eph 6:18)*. We do this at specific times set aside exclusively for prayer and we also do it at fleeting moments during the day as we spontaneously lift our minds to God with thoughts of praise, thanksgiving or petition.

Sometimes we pray in private, as our Lord instructed us *(cf. Mt 6:6)* and at other times we join in a community prayer as the Apostles did in the upper room *(cf. Acts 1:14)*. Our Lord instructed us to pray together when He instituted the Eucharist and said, "do this in memory of me" *(Lk 22:19)* and He told us that, "where two or three are gathered together in my name, there am I in the midst of them" *(Mt 18:20)*. But He also left us an example of the need for private prayer. Luke tells us that Jesus often went off to the Mount of Olives to pray *(cf. Lk 21:37; 22:39; 6:12)* and His forty days in the desert was a solitary retreat. Peter and Paul, both so active in the community of the early Church, also retreated for personal private prayer *(cf. Acts 10:9; Gal 1:16-17)*.

Whether private or community oriented there is a strong calling for a Christian to become a person of prayer. But that prayerfulness is not normally automatic or totally spontaneous. There is a need to develop a habit of regular prayer, an attitude of prayerfulness that is best developed during the formative years of youth in the loving atmosphere of the family. It is for this reason that we have established several family prayer practices within our family. It is our hope and prayer that by sharing some of our experiences, others will be prompted to try some of our suggestions in their own families as well as being encouraged to experiment and develop prayer practices of their own choosing.

II

Grace Before Meals

The shared family meal is the most basic and potentially the most unifying of all family gatherings. From earliest times a shared meal has been a special sign of friendship and unity. Even today we still find a shared meal as the central event in most family gatherings and special occasions. It might be an annual family reunion, Christmas dinner with all the trimmings or perhaps a birthday celebration. Often a mother will make an extra effort to fix a favorite dish in honor of her child's birthday. Or think of the excitement and anticipation of Thanksgiving Day when so many families return home for that special family gathering. And what would that traditional family gathering be without a meal? Whether the meal be fancy or simple, whether it be a full-course dinner or mid-morning coffee, there is something special and almost sacred about sharing it with another. One's food is basic to sustaining one's existence and when one shares one's food with another it is very much like sharing one's life with another.

For the Christian family, the shared meal is more than just a gathering of people who have a special feeling for

5

each other. It is more than just a sharing of sustenance. It is an opportunity to bring our Lord and Savior Jesus Christ into the midst of the family. Jesus said, "where two or three are gathered together in my name, there am I in the midst of them" *(Mt 18:20)*. What better time than this to acknowledge Him and ask Him to be with us? We know from reading the Scriptures that Jesus often shared a meal with His closest friends and also with the multitudes that followed Him. He was a guest at the home of the tax collector Zacchaeus *(cf. Lk 19:5)* and He dined with Martha and Mary *(cf. Lk 10:38)*. He provided repast for the multitudes *(cf. Lk 9:16)* and greatly desired to eat the Passover meal with His disciples *(cf. Lk 22:15)*. He was often accused by the Pharisees of eating with sinners *(cf. Lk 5:30; 19:7)* and He will join us at table if we will only ask Him. He who provides for all of our meals waits for an invitation; how sad it is that so few families take the fifteen to twenty seconds required to say a table grace and offer that invitation.

The practice of saying grace at mealtime has been a Christian tradition from Apostolic times, being probably a natural carry-over from the even earlier Jewish tradition. It was customary for our Lord to offer thanks before meals *(cf. Jn 6:11; Mk 6:41; 8:6; Mt 15:36)* and Luke tells us in Acts 27:35 that Paul "took bread, gave thanks to God . . . and began to eat."

Many of the early Church Fathers attest to the universal custom of grace before meals. Early in the second century the apologist Aristides declared of his fellow Christians that, "Over their food and over their drink they render God thanks" and Tertullian proclaimed, "We do not recline at a banquet before prayer be first tasted." Clement of Alexandria tells us, "Before taking nourishment it is fitting to praise the Creator of all things and it is fitting also to sing His praises when we take as nourishment the things created by Him." There is evidence that this tradition continued through many centuries and it is only in our own "modern and sophisticated" era that Christians cannot find the time to praise the Lord at meals. Even among regular church-going Christians, table grace seems to have diminished.

And yet the practice has not disappeared completely. Many will still ask a blessing on special occasions such as Thanksgiving Day or Christmas. This was my own experience as I grew up. It was not until I was on my own and married that grace before meals became a regular daily practice in our home. When we first began the practice of saying grace it was a very private thing. If we were having company we would forego it; we did not want to "embarrass" our company (or perhaps ourselves). We did not want to give the impression that we were trying to show off a "false holiness."

As we became more comfortable in ourselves, we gradually began to say grace with company present. Now we observe the opposite effect—when we visit people who have been at our home they sometimes ask us to say grace in their home.

Table grace is such a simple thing, and yet for many people it is psychologically difficult for a variety of reasons. It might be a certain self-consciousness about sharing openly a faith they perceive as very personal or private; it might be a fear of an implied commitment which would require changes in other areas of one's life; or perhaps the idea has never presented itself before. Whatever the reason, it can be overcome with a simple resolution and determination.

The actual practice of saying grace is quite simple and may be varied according to the needs of the family. The head of the family may lead, it can be said together as a group or the lead may be varied from day to day. The prayer may be personal and spontaneous or it can be one that is pre-defined. The traditional Catholic form is as follows:

Bless us, O Lord, and these Thy gifts,
which we are about to receive, from Thy bounty,
through Christ our Lord. Amen.

Another which we have used on occasion was given to us by Father Randal Gillette, C.P., on one of his many visits to our home.

Bless this food, heavenly Father,
which You have given us in Your mercy.
May it bring us strength to work in Your service.
Forgive us our sins and lead all men back to You.
We offer You our prayer through Christ our Savior
and Lord. Amen.

This slightly longer table grace was also given to us by Father Gillette:

Loving Father,
We thank You for gathering us together for this meal.
May we continue to live in Your friendship
and harmony with one another.
Bless this food, which You give us as a sign of Your
loving care for us, and bless us in our daily lives.
Bless Your Church throughout the world,
and all those who seek to do Your will today.
Father of mercy, all praise be to You
through Jesus Christ our Savior, in the unity of
the Holy Spirit, one God, for ever and ever. Amen.

Although grace before meals was not a regular part of my growing up, my father would ask a blessing on those special occasions such as Thanksgiving and Christmas or, in later years, when the family came together for a special event. He would generally thank the Lord that those dear to him were with him again and then say something like:

We thank You Lord for
this food on the table.
Bless it to our use
and us to Thy service. Amen.

A prayer that we have used on occasion when we have had friends (or relatives) with us to share the meal is:

*We thank You Lord for all the
blessings You have bestowed
upon us; for the food upon the
table and friends (family) here
to share it with us. Amen.*

There are many others which you can use. Or you can create your own. There is even a book, *Table Graces for the Family,* selected by Marjorie Ingzel and published by Thomas Nelson Inc., which is filled with table graces. Traditional graces from other countries and for special occasions are included as well as several appropriate Bible verses. Another source of table graces is *Catholic Household Blessings and Prayers,* published by the National Conference of Catholic Bishops, which contains a variety of mealtime prayers.

III

Parents Are Teachers

During the past quarter century, we have seen a profound change in the position of Catholic parents in the religious education process. That position has changed from "tutor" to "left out" to "primary educator." In the days of the Baltimore Catechism prior to Vatican II, the technique used to teach the facts of the Faith was primarily the memorization of pre-defined answers to pre-defined questions. The students learned *the facts* but sadly, many times did not understand the significance or application to real-life situations.

In this method, everything was clear and well organized. The children knew exactly what was expected of them, as did their parents. At the very least, the parents were expected to ensure that the child spent adequate time memorizing. Thus the parent became somewhat of a policeman. If the parents wanted to do more, they could sit down with the child, ask the questions and monitor the answers, perhaps offering some explanations or practical suggestions along the way. Thus the parent became the tutor.

This dual role of tutor and policeman could be very comfortable; it didn't require any thinking or planning. You simply picked up the book, read the proper question and compared the verbal response to the written answer. In spite of all the obvious drawbacks, there was at least one important benefit: Because it was so easy, parents could participate in the process and give the child their undivided attention. This attention could very subtly remind the child of two very important facts: 1) the parent was interested in the child and 2) the parent considered religious education important.

In the wake of Vatican II, all of this was drastically changed. Religious educators and text book publishers became aware of two revolutionary concepts: 1) Vatican II's call for renewal in the Church by refocusing on the basic Christian message and 2) the memorization of *facts* did not necessarily prepare one to live an active Christian life. The old methods were quickly, abruptly and almost universally scrapped. With this profound change of direction came a genuine sense of frustration for many parents. They were not sure what the new programs were trying to teach, and it was not always apparent what type of participation was expected of them. Although Vatican II declared parents to be the primary educators (and often the new texts contained instructions for the parents), many still felt left out of a process they had not asked for and did not fully understand.

Others were equally frustrated but for a different reason. Many people perceived a lack of substance in many of the new programs; after several years of instruction the students often did not know the Ten Commandments, the precepts of the Church, the beatitudes or any number of other "important facts." I have known parents who actually pulled their children out of the CCD program and taught them at home. There were times when I too felt the same temptation, but realized we are called to be part of a community. How could we be a part of that community if we divorced ourselves from it? We opted instead to supplement the program with a certain amount of home instruction.

In recent years, educators have begun to evaluate the successes and failures of the new programs. The result has been an increasing emphasis on the role of parents. There is a general realization that forty-five minutes a week of CCD class is just not enough; living a Christian life is a full time calling. Parents are being urged to participate more active-ly. In many parishes it is now customary for the parents to attend instructional sessions when their children are being prepared for the reception of the sacraments. Catholic mag-azine and newspaper articles regularly urge parents to assume their proper role as primary religious educators. Equally evident has been the call for what is termed fami-ly spirituality; families praying and sharing their faith together.

I believe there is no better place for children to learn to live a Christian life than in the security of their home. Although this may seem like a new idea, it is in fact older than Christianity itself. In Chapters 12 and 13 of the book of Exodus, we find the story of the institution of the Jewish feast of Passover, which was to be celebrated each year in perpetuity. Even to this day, 3,000 years later, Jewish fami-lies still gather together each year to recall that event. Fol-lowing the directives of Moses, this celebration includes a religious education session that recalls the significance of the event. The education takes place painlessly and effec-tively in the loving environment of a shared meal within the security of the family.

We too can adopt this technique in the teaching of our own children. My wife and I have found mealtime to be an ideal time to share our religious faith with our children and have developed a year-round program which allows us to focus on a variety of religious truths and traditional devotions.

In what we have termed a mealtime prayer-learning experience we introduce a specific theme for each month or liturgical season. Each mealtime prayer-learning experience includes an informal instruction session which is reinforced with a daily commemoration when we say grace before meals. This combination of monthly theme and daily commemoration provides an effective combination of variety and repetition. The longer instruction sessions vary from month to month and are relatively infrequent, while the daily repetitive commemoration provides a short, painless reminder of the lesson. In subsequent chapters I will describe the background and practices which we follow throughout the year. But I would first like to point out that it is more important for a family to pray and share together than it is to follow a particular format. It is not expected that every family will be attracted to all of the practices that we have used. I do hope, however, that some of our experiences will be of benefit to all.

Our mealtime prayer-learning experiences evolved over a period of many years. In the early years of our marriage we used the same simple form of grace before meals without variation or additions.

Our earliest addition was the Advent wreath. During the first several years we used the home ceremony found in the booklet *Family Advent Customs* by Helen McLaughlin (Liturgical Press, 1954). In later years we used the Advent prayers from the December edition of the monthly missalette. Both of these are short and caused no resistance among the children in their younger years. As the children got older we added Scripture readings and prayers with a definite theme for each week of Advent. These additions have enhanced both the learning experience and spiritual development aspects of our Advent celebration.

May devotions were another early addition, with others added somewhat irregularly over the years. Sometimes as we began a new month I would ask if anyone knew what (traditional) devotion was associated with the new month. Invariably, one of the children would run for the Catholic dictionary and come back with the answer which we would then use as a cue for an instructional session. As the years went by, we began to increase the instructional sessions and add specific commemorations for the various months. We would generally hold the discussion after dinner on the first or second Sunday of the month when the whole family could gather without having to rush away for outside activities or homework. We have varied the format from year to year, omitting or shortening the discussion if the older children were familiar with the subject and the youngest was not ready yet.

Each of the following chapters describes a devotion associated with a particular month or season. All of these devotions provide opportunities for learning experiences and the presentation of Christian teachings. In each discussion I have included background information and key catechetical thoughts as well as a description of our mealtime prayers, which vary from simple one-line additions to longer family prayer services.

While the discussions may be held at any time, we preferred mealtime for several reasons: The mealtime setting creates a positive link to the daily repetition of the monthly or seasonal commemoration which is included with grace before meals; there is a certain unity of spirit that is fostered around the dinner table when we invite the Lord to be an unseen guest; and we found it easier to keep everyone together after mealtime than to schedule a separate session which would compete with other activities.

Many of the longer prayers may be inappropriate for families who have not previously prayed together in the home. For example, if a family that has never said grace at mealtime suddenly begins to read long Scripture passages before dinner they may find that their (hungry) children become upset and disinterested. This became apparent from the comments of several families who tried our Advent program. Some who had a history of shared family prayer would have welcomed more while others said the program was too long for their family.

Better to begin in a less ambitious way than to risk a backlash of disinterest and resistance. For example, the family could begin to say grace regularly and wait until the following year before adding longer devotions. The Advent wreath might be used with short prayers for the first year or two. Young children generally enjoy the candle lighting if the prayers and readings are not too long. The longer readings and prayers may be added when the family is ready. The most important thing is to begin; supplements can always be added later.

Finally, before we look at the various devotions, I'd like to add a note to members of other Christian denominations: Many of these devotions and teachings will appear to be decidedly Roman Catholic in nature; that is because we are Catholic and this book reflects our own unique family experiences. I invite you to read through all of the chapters and thus gain a better understanding of many of our beliefs and practices. Some will fit your family situation while others will not, but certainly the idea of a shared family prayer-learning experience is valid for families of all faiths.

May our Lord and Savior Jesus Christ be with you all as you begin (or continue) to pray and learn together as a family.

IV

December

Month of Advent and the Nativity

We begin our discussion of monthly devotions with December because the Advent season which begins the Church year occurs mostly, and in some years entirely, in December.

Advent is a time of spiritual preparation for the coming of the Lord at Christmas. It begins on the fourth Sunday before Christmas. This period of waiting and preparation recalls the centuries of anticipation as the Israelites waited and prayed for the coming of the Messiah.

The origins of Advent as a period of special preparation for Christmas reach back to the beginning of the fifth century. Historically it has been a strict penitential season which included prayer and fasting. In recent years, the emphasis has shifted from penance and fasting to prayer and spiritual preparation for a closer relationship with the Lord at Christmas.

There are many helpful customs and traditions which may be used to great advantage in spiritual preparation for the feast of Christmas. The Advent calendar is particularly appealing to younger children who love to open the little doors to find the various pictures or messages. The observance of Saint Nicholas Day can help to offset some of the commercialism of Santa Claus, and of course the traditional Christmas creche reminds us of the true meaning of Christmas. But perhaps the most popular custom in recent years is the Advent wreath which we increasingly find in both home and church.

The Advent wreath had its beginning some 400 years ago among the Protestants of Eastern Germany. It is a Christian adaptation of the ancient pagan practice of lighting candles and fires at the winter solstice. From very early times, the Church has used candles as an integral part of Christian worship, and the idea of converting the traditional Yule candles into Advent candles representing Christ as the "Light of the World" is understandable and indeed fortunate. The practice spread quickly throughout Germany and was in a sense an ecumenical custom, inasmuch as it was accepted in both Catholic and Protestant homes.

The Advent wreath was slower to take hold in America. Only thirty or forty years ago it was relatively unknown in this country. Today it is fast becoming one of the most popular symbols of the Christmas season.

The celebration of Advent and the making of an Advent wreath have been part of our family's Christmas preparation for many years. During those years we have attempted to make the Advent season and the use of the Advent wreath a learning experience as well as a prayer experience for our children. It can be a delightful and rewarding experience for all.

Making an Advent wreath is not difficult. You begin with a wire ring to which are attached four candleholders. The ring can be homemade or easily purchased at a religious goods store. Each item in the Advent wreath has special significance and acts as an aid in explaining the meaning of Advent. The continuous circle represents the living and eternal God who has no beginning and no end.

The circle is covered with evergreens. We have used artificial greens, but when convenient we prefer the fragrance and beauty of real fresh greens. The evergreens represent the unchanging nature of God, while the color green symbolizes the hope of springtime and new life. A little red (ribbon or holly berries) may be added to remind us of the blood which Christ shed for us.

The flame from the candles represents Christ, the Light of the World. One candle is lit during the first week and each Sunday another candle is lit until the fourth week, when all four candles are lit. The increasing number of candles represents the increasing brightness of the light of salvation as we approach the Savior's birth.

The color of the candles is also significant. Three of the candles are purple, in keeping with the penitential nature of the Advent season. The fourth candle (which is lit on the third Sunday) is rose-colored (or sometimes pink) and represents the joy which is building up as we approach the time of the Savior at Christmas. In recent years some people have used blue candles in place of the purple to contrast the hopefulness of Advent with the strict penitential season of Lent.

We have used several different devotional exercises over the years, but as the children have grown older and their attention span has increased, we have included various Scriptural selections which retell the story of God's plan of salvation. This story begins with the fall of man in the Garden of Eden, proceeds through the centuries of promise and preparation and culminates in the birth of our Lord and Savior. We try in this sequence, to capture and in a sense relive Israel's waiting and longing for the Messiah. In this way we can better appreciate the significance of the event we celebrate on Christmas Day.

In the first week of Advent we concentrate on God's creation and man's rejection of God's plan for happiness. We have chosen readings and prayers which help us call to mind our own sinfulness and rejection of God's love. We try to see and understand those areas of our lives which need to be transformed through the grace of God.

In the second week we begin to look at God's promise of salvation. We look at some of the early prophecies and see the promise and expectation to which the Israelites clung through several centuries. Through good times and bad, hope and expectation survived. They must have truly been the Chosen People and specially blessed by God to have held on to such a distant promise for so long without despair or loss of hope.

Finally, the promise becomes clearer and the expectation of fulfillment becomes almost universal among the Jewish nation. It is these unmistakable prophetic pointers to Jesus Christ which we examine in the third week of Advent. We come to appreciate the miracle that God provided through His prophets. Before the event happened He foretold what was to take place. The circumstances of His birth, including His birthplace, His mission of peace and healing, even the suffering and rejection He would undergo, are clearly recorded.

In the fourth week we pick up the theme of John the Baptist to *Prepare the way of the Lord*. The *advent* or *coming* of the Savior is close at hand. We continue our final preparations as we pray: "Lord Jesus, as we approach this Christmas season, come into our hearts and remain with us always."

On Christmas Day we rejoice in the birth of our Lord and Savior Jesus Christ. In the days that immediately follow Christmas, we recall the birth and manifestation of Christ to the world as we read selected portions of the four Gospels.

Our complete Advent program, including daily readings, weekly responsorial prayers and comments can be found in Appendix A2.

V

January

Month of the Holy Name of Jesus

C hristianity, whose roots reach back into Judaism, can trace a long and very ancient tradition of praise and honor for the Name of the Lord. The second of the Ten Commandments as recorded in both Exodus *(20:7)* and Deuteronomy *(5:11)* says "You shall not take the name of the LORD, your God, in vain."

The Old Testament Jews were so in awe of the Holy Name of the Lord that they would not even speak it. They would write it or think it but they would not be so bold as to presume they were worthy to speak the Name of Yahweh. They had great reverence and respect for God and an awesome fear of the Lord. There was no other god like their God and they would honor His Name. This tradition of honoring the Holy Name of the Lord is evident in many of the Psalms *(cf. Ps 92:1; 103:1; 113:1-3; 135:1-3: 145:1-2).*

Jesus modified this outlook somewhat when He taught us to call God "Our Father" or "Abba" which many translate into the very familiar "daddy." Jesus was not teaching us to be disrespectful but only showing us that God loves us dearly and that we should approach Him as a child approaches a loving father. Jesus tells us that God, our Father, loves us and wants us to come to Him in both pain and joy and to be on friendly, familiar terms with Him and He will make everything all right.

Yes, Jesus changed the human relationship to God, but there is still room for reverence for God's Holy Name and the Holy Name of His Son Jesus, whom we Christians proclaim as the second person of the Blessed Trinity and God co-eternal with the Father. And so it is that January is the Month of the Holy Name of Jesus; a time to think about Jesus and to make a resolution to honor His Holy Name.

Paul tells us in his letter to the Phillipians that God highly exalted Him, giving Him a Name above every other name so that every knee must bend at the Name of Jesus *(cf. Phil 2:9-10)*.

In my childhood I remember being told that we should bow our heads when we hear the Name of Jesus. To this day that custom remains. When I hear the Name of Jesus whether reverently, or irreverently, I instinctively (though ever so slightly) nod my head. If the reference to the Name of Jesus is reverent my nod becomes a prayer of praise; for the irreverent reference, it is a silent prayer of reparation.

During the month of January, when we gather together and recite our grace before meals, we add this short prayer: Praised be the Name of Jesus our Lord and Savior. Thus our mealtime blessing becomes:

Bless us, O Lord, and these Thy gifts,
which we are about to receive, from Thy bounty,
through Christ our Lord. Amen.
Praised be the Name of Jesus our Lord and Savior. Amen.

We also suggest the Litany of the Holy Name of Jesus as an after-meal prayer sometime during the month. The Litany can be a valuable teaching tool as we consider the meaning behind the various titles of our Lord.

Before we leave this subject of the Holy Name of Jesus, there is one more thing to be offered for consideration and reflection. The Book of Exodus *(Ex 23:13)* says, "Never mention the name of any other god; it shall not be heard from your lips."

This command was given in a time when pagan peoples all around the Jews worshiped many and varied gods. There was a strong temptation and tendency on the part of the Jews to look with favor on these false gods, and so it was that God told them they should not even mention the name of any other gods.

This command may seem to have little relevance for us today when you consider that we live in a country and culture where people do not believe in more than one God. While there are some who believe in no God and forms of worship may vary, the days of multiple pagan gods seem to be gone. But, consider for a moment the neo-paganism of our time.

Consider how we from time to time are tempted to put material goods and pleasure before God. Don't we sometimes almost make gods of money, cars, house, career, education, vacation, clothes, personal appearance, the "right" kind of friends, and so on? All of these things in their proper perspective are good and necessary, but we must guard against them becoming central to our lives.

During the month of January, let us ponder and praise the Name of Jesus and ask ourselves if we really and truly consider Jesus to be the central focal point of our lives. Let us resolve always to strive to make Jesus number one in our lives and strive fully to do His will, remembering with John the Baptist that "He must increase; I must decrease" *(Jn 3:30)*.

Praised be the Holy Name of Jesus in the month of January, and always.

VI

February

Month of the Passion

The Passion and death of our Lord is one of Christianity's most significant historical happenings and one of the principal mysteries of our Faith. It is through the suffering and death of Jesus on the Cross that we are redeemed and saved; as Paul tells us in his letter to the Ephesians, we have been redeemed and our sins forgiven through His Blood (*cf. Eph 1:7*).

The events and sufferings of our Lord's Passion have since earliest times provided the saints and mystics with the subject of many meditations. We too can benefit from time spent pondering the meaning of the Passion of our Lord and the love that God manifests for us when He gives His only begotten Son that we might have life everlasting. Two different stories of the Passion provide insights and meditation aids as we consider the suffering of our Lord.

Most of our familiarity with the Passion comes from the Gospel stories, but there is another story which was written hundreds of years before the birth of Christ. It is taken from the Old Testament and combines selections from Psalm 22 and the prophet Isaiah. The "suffering servant" song of Isaiah provides a vivid, prophetic picture of our Lord's suffering more than 500 years before the event, while Psalm 22, beginning with the words of abandonment which our Lord repeated on the Cross, reveals the inner anguish of one unjustly persecuted.

Lord, how you have helped me before! You took me safely from my mother's womb and brought me through the years of infancy. I have depended upon you since birth; you have always been my God. Don't leave me now, for trouble is near and no one else can possibly help.

I am surrounded by fearsome enemies, strong as the giant bulls from Bashan. They come at me with open jaws, like roaring lions attacking their prey. *(Ps 22:9-13 TLB)*

He was oppressed and he was afflicted, yet he never said a word. He was brought as a lamb to the slaughter; and as a sheep before her shearers is dumb, so he stood silent before the ones condemning him. *(Is 53:7 TLB)*

We despised him and rejected him—a man of sorrows, acquainted with bitterest grief. We turned our backs on him and looked the other way when he went by. He was despised and we didn't care. *(Is 53:3 TLB)*

But I am a worm, not a man, scorned and despised by my own people and by all mankind. Everyone who sees me mocks and sneers and shrugs. *(Ps 22:6-7 TLB)*

I give my back to the whip, and my cheeks to those who pull out the beard. I do not hide from shame—they spit in my face. *(Is 50:6 TLB)*

Yet it was *our* grief he bore, *our* sorrows that weighed him down. And we thought his troubles were a punishment from God, for his *own* sins! But he was wounded and bruised for *our* sins. He was chastised that we might have peace; he was lashed—and we were healed! *We* are the ones who strayed away like sheep! *We,* who left God's paths to follow our own. Yet God laid on *him* the guilt and sins of every one of us! *(Is 53:4-6 TLB)*

My strength has drained away like water, and all my bones are out of joint. My heart melts like wax; my strength has dried up like sun-baked clay; my tongue sticks to my mouth, for you have laid me in the dust of death. The enemy, this gang of evil men, circles me like a pack of dogs; they have pierced my hands and feet. I can count every bone in my body. See these men of evil gloat and stare; they divide my clothes among themselves by a toss of the dice. *(Ps 22:14-18 TLB)*

My God, My God, why have you forsaken me? Why do you refuse to help me or even to listen to my groans? Day and night I keep on weeping, crying for your help, but there is no reply—for *you are holy.*
The praises of our fathers surrounded your throne; they trusted you and you delivered them. You heard their cries for help and saved them; they were never disappointed when they sought your aid. *(Ps 22:1-5 TLB)*

"Is this the one who rolled his burden on the Lord?" they laugh. "Is this the one who claims the Lord delights in him? We'll believe it when we see God rescue him!" *(Ps 22:8 TLB)*

Because the Lord God helps me, I will not be dismayed; therefore, I have set my face like flint to do his will, and I know that I will triumph. *(Is 50:7 TLB)*

Yet it was the Lord's good plan to bruise him and fill him with grief. But when his soul has been made an offering for sin, then he shall have a multitude of children, many heirs. He shall live again and God's program shall prosper in his hands. And when he sees all that is accomplished by the anguish of his soul, he shall be satisfied; and because of what he has experienced, my righteous

Servant shall make many to be counted righteous before God, for he shall bear all their sins. Therefore I will give him the honors of one who is mighty and great, because he has poured out his soul unto death. He was counted as a sinner, and he bore the sins of many, and he pled with God for sinners. *(Is 53:10-12 TLB)*

From prison and trial they led him away to his death. But who among the people of that day realized it was their sins that he was dying for—that he was suffering their punishment? He was buried like a criminal in a rich man's grave; but he had done no wrong, and had never spoken an evil word. *(Is 53:8-9 TLB)*

Yet many shall be amazed when they see him—yes, even far-off foreign nations and their kings; they shall stand dumfounded, speechless in his presence. For they shall see and understand what they had not been told before. They shall see my Servant beaten and bloodied, so disfigured one would scarcely know it was a person standing there. So shall he cleanse many nations. *(Is 52:14-15 TLB)*

Our second story of the Passion of our Lord is based on a medical and historical examination of the Gospel accounts. The historical descriptions of Roman crucifixion provide insight into the physical torture that our Lord endured. Add to this a medical perspective and we get a vivid picture of an ordeal so horrible that Dr. Pierre Barbet in his book *A Doctor at Calvary* (Doubleday—Image Books 1963) reported he could no longer do the Stations of the Cross. It was Dr. Barbet who gave us an incredible medical analysis of the Passion based on his study of the Shroud of Turin, which contains an unmistakable image of a crucified man who had been scourged and crowned with thorns.

Until recently the Shroud was widely accepted as the authentic burial cloth of Jesus. Extensive twentieth century scientific studies had led many to conclude that the question was no longer one of authenticity but rather one of how the image appeared on the cloth. The 1988 carbon-dating tests, however, have indicated that the material is not old enough to have been the linen burial cloth mentioned in the Gospels. This most recent test actually creates more questions than answers, as scientists attempt to determine the origin of an image that was not painted and appears as a photographic negative. Some have seriously questioned the validity of the 1988 tests and have called for new ones. Despite the questions and mystery surrounding the Shroud, one thing is certain: The image is one of extraordinary detail and provides a vivid icon of our Lord's Passion. Dr. Barbet's study found every detail to be consistent with the Gospel reports, historical knowledge of crucifixion from Roman times and his own knowledge of anatomy and physiology. His findings are reported in great depth in *A Doctor at Calvary*. I consider this work to be the best available for acquiring a greater insight into the physical Passion of Jesus.

Prior knowledge of a dire event can be the cause of stress and great mental anguish, so that the suffering of the actual unhappy (physical) occurrence is preceded by weeks, months or even years of mental suffering. Consider, for example, the diagnosis of a terminal illness which may not yet be causing much physical pain; or the experience of a mother whose son is scheduled to participate in an imminent military invasion.

We do not know at what age Jesus (in His human nature) became fully aware of His eventual fate, but there is ample Scriptural evidence of considerable prior knowledge. Saint Luke tells us that even at the tender age of twelve, Jesus was aware that He was to have a special mission in life *(cf. Lk 2:42-49)*. His Jewish upbringing would certainly have included a study of the Scriptures and indeed we know from the Gospel of Luke that Jesus was familiar with the prophet Isaiah *(cf. Lk 4:14-21)*. He correctly interpreted chapter 61 of Isaiah and there is no reason to think He was not equally familiar with Isaiah 53 or Psalm 22.

Matthew *(cf. 16:21; 17:22-23)*, Mark *(cf. 8:31; 9:31)*, Luke *(cf. 9:22)* and John *(cf. 7:33; 12:23-32; 16:5-16)* all tell us of Jesus' prior knowledge of His Passion and death. This prior knowledge reached a climax in the garden of Gethsemane, where, as Mark tells us, He was "troubled and distressed" *(Mk 14:33)* and as Luke tells us "He was in such agony and he prayed so fervently that his sweat became like drops of blood" *(Lk 22:44). Stedman's Medical Dictionary* defines a condition known as hematidrosis as "excretion of blood or blood pigment in the sweat." This is an extremely rare disorder brought on by grave mental anguish and emotional strain. Jesus suffered this emotional strain as He thought about His impending ordeal and contemplated the significance of His actions. He must have been fully and totally aware that He (who had not sinned) was about to take on the guilt of humanity and offer satisfaction for the sins of all mankind. Jesus was truly divine; but He was also fully human, like us in all things save sin. He was almost overwhelmed with grief as He said "My soul is sorrowful even to death" *(Mk 14:34)*. The condition (hematidrosis) which resulted from this emotional strain also precipitated a very significant effect of its own: the entire surface of His sacred body became extremely sensitive to pain. This sensitivity thus magnifies all that is to happen that evening and the next day.

Jesus is then arrested like a common criminal, deserted by His friends and disciples and subjected to all manner of verbal abuse, which He suffers in silence. His accusers convict Him with false testimony and trumped-up charges and next morning hand Him over to Pilate for sentencing and punishment.

Pilate senses the innocence of Jesus but is fearful that his reluctant subjects may stir up trouble. He decides first to have Jesus scourged and then released. Scourging in itself was a fearful sentence and consisted of more than just the lash. The victim was given over to the soldiers for all kinds of cruel punishment and mockery, as may have been suggested by the nature of the crime. In the case of Jesus, who was accused of claiming to be a king and prophet, it would have been quite natural for the soldiers to mock Him as a king and at the same time treat Him as anything but royalty. They put a purple robe on Him and bowed before Him in mock homage, then spit on Him and beat Him with fists and sticks. The impression on the Holy Shroud which was examined so closely by Dr. Barbet shows clear evidence of a broken nose, which could have resulted from one of the blows. Finally, as a king the soldiers give Him a crown; not a royal crown but a crown of thorns.

If you remember for a moment when you have picked roses or blackberries and been pricked by a thorn, you know the sharp pain that can be caused by a single thorn. The thorns in Jesus' crown would have been just as sharp, but even longer than rose thorns. The crown was fashioned in such a way as to cover the entire scalp. After it was placed on His head the soldiers beat on it with sticks to ensure that the thorns bit into the scalp. As we consider His pain and suffering, we should remember that this was a <u>human</u> body which had been rendered supersensitive to pain as a result of the condition of hematidrosis.

When the soldiers finally tired of their mockery and amusement, they took Jesus off for the actual scourging. Jewish law limited scourging to forty lashes and the Pharisees would only go to thirty-nine in order to ensure that they did not break the law; but Jesus was scourged by Roman soldiers whose law had no such restriction. The whip which was used in the scourging would have had two leather thongs attached to a handle and would have had bits of bone or metal fastened to the ends. Dr. Barbet's study of the Shroud suggests that two soldiers participated in the scourging. They would have continued the scourging until they were too tired to continue. We do not know how many lashes Jesus actually received. Dr. Barbet reports that he was able to count about 120 marks on the Shroud suggesting that Jesus had been lashed at least sixty times. It is conceivable that He endured many more blows.

Jesus is now brought back to Pilate for the infamous *Ecce Homo* ("Behold, the man!" *(Jn 19:5)*) scene in which Pilate again presents Jesus to the crowd in hopes of releasing Him. But they cry out "Crucify him!" *(Jn 19:15)*.

Jesus was led away and made to carry His Cross. There is much symbolism associated with the Cross: The carrying of one's own cross has long been symbolic of accepting life's day-to-day trials and tribulations in the spirit of conformity to God's will. The Cross which Jesus carried has been seen to represent the sins of all mankind.

It is not, however, the symbolism that we address here but rather Jesus' actual physical suffering. The carrying of the Cross is usually pictured with a complete cross in the form of a "†", but historians generally believe that one who was to be crucified would be made to carry the crossbeam, while the upright shaft would already be in place at the crucifixion site. It is likely then that Jesus was made to carry a heavy wooden beam somewhat smaller than a railroad tie

and weighing perhaps a hundred pounds or more. Carrying such an object any distance would be an ordeal for one who was well rested. Jesus must already have been near exhaustion. He would have been fatigued, having had little or no sleep the night before, weakened from loss of blood, and his entire body was filled with physical and emotional pain resulting from Gethsemane and the scourging. Having a heavy, rough-hewn beam put on a shoulder already torn by pain must have been an almost intolerable burden.

Tradition tells us that Jesus fell three times under the weight of the Cross and each time He got up to continue His mission of salvation and set an example for us as we carry our symbolic cross through life. If you consider the traditional Stations of the Cross, can it be accidental or is it divine guidance that caused the Church to depict three of them identically? Surely many other scenes could have been depicted. Perhaps it is so that we who fall so often can be inspired to rise each time and continue on through life to our own glorious reunion with the Father and our loved ones who have gone before us.

As we continue to examine the physical sufferings, we should consider the consequences of a fall under a heavy weight. Jesus would have been forced hard to the ground; His knees would have been bloodied; the roughness of the beam would have driven splinters into His shoulder; the wounds from the scourging would have reopened and deepened, causing additional suffering to that already tormented body.

So great was His anguish that the soldiers, experienced executioners, were afraid He would die along the way. The soldiers then forced Simon the Cyrenian to assist in the walk to Calvary. Here again we have opportunity for meditation as we consider our response to the symbolic call to carry (in union with Jesus) our own cross through life.

As they reach Calvary Jesus is stripped of His garments. Again, old wounds reopen where blood has dried and stuck to His clothing. His arms are then stretched out parallel to the crossbeam and huge nails are driven through His wrists into the beam. The nails would have been driven through His wrists and not the hands as popularly pictured because the hands could not have supported the body's weight. The point at which the nails were driven into His wrists is an extremely sensitive nerve center which would have resulted in additional excruciating pain. The crossbeam, with Jesus fastened to it, was then lifted up and put in place. His feet were then nailed to the upright.

At this point, the pain and suffering are almost unimaginable, but the real ordeal in crucifixion is one of breathing. The body's weight presses on the lungs and one can only breath by pulling one's weight up against the nails, the wounds and the severed nerves in the wrists. Jesus remained in this unbelievable condition for three hours, continuing to exhibit His love and compassion for others, asking forgiveness for His executioners (cf. Lk 23:34) and promising eternal life to one of the thieves crucified with

Him *(cf. Lk 23:43)*. Here again there is a lesson for us to learn: Although we are bound to do good works *(cf. Jas 2:14-26)* it is not the *quantity* of our good works that earn salvation but rather the mercifulness and love of God. In fact, we do not *earn* salvation at all. It is a free gift from a loving Father, if we will just repent and believe and accept His love. The thief on the cross had no further opportunity to perform works; he merely asked Jesus in faith to remember him and became the only person that we know who was actually and personally assured of salvation by the words of our Lord Himself.

After three hours on the Cross, Jesus dies and all appears to be over; His enemies seem to have won. Considering the ordeal we have just described, there should be no doubt that Jesus really died, but there is one more incident which erases all doubt: A soldier thrusts a spear deep into His side, piercing His heart and removing all shadow of doubt.

All seems lost at this point, and His followers are scattered. But after the agony and despair comes the glory of the Resurrection. The New Covenant and the Resurrection have made Christianity a religion of joy and hope, but to fully appreciate the joy of the Resurrection it is necessary to experience the grief of the Cross.

During the month of February we try to give our children a deeper understanding of the Passion. We discuss the Old and New Testament stories after Sunday dinner during the first couple weeks of February. We also add an acknowledgment of the Passion to our February grace before meals so that the blessing becomes:

Bless us, O Lord, and these Thy gifts,
which we are about to receive,
from Thy bounty, through Christ our Lord
who has suffered so much for us. Amen.

VII

The Lenten Season

Saint Paul tells us "those who belong to Christ [Jesus] have crucified their flesh with its passions and desires" *(Gal 5:24)* and in his first letter to the Corinthians Paul tells us he disciplines his own body "for fear that, after having preached to others, I myself should be disqualified" *(1 Cor 9:27)*.

Each year the Church gives us a similar reminder as we are called to observe the penitential season of Lent. The Lenten tradition, a period of spiritual preparation for the glorious feast of Easter, traces its beginnings back to Apostolic times. In the early years, there was considerable variety in both the form and length of the observance, but as early as the beginning of the fourth century we find evidence of an almost universal custom of a forty-day period of prayer and fasting. The forty-day period is in keeping with the example of our Lord, who went into the desert for forty days of prayer and fasting in preparation for his public ministry.

The principal teaching method employed by our Lord was the spoken word, but He also showed us much by His

35

own personal example. This is particularly true of His retreat to the solitude of the desert. Jesus had known from an early age that He was different and that He had a special purpose and mission *(cf. Lk 2:49)* but He also continued to gain wisdom as He advanced in age *(cf. Lk 2:52)*. In His human nature He had to learn and gradually come to appreciate the full impact of who He was. Shortly before the beginning of His public ministry Jesus came to John to be baptized "and the holy Spirit descended upon him . . . a voice came from heaven, 'You are my beloved Son; with you I am well pleased'" *(Lk 3:22)*.

With this new revelation, Jesus gained even greater insight into His Messianic mission and probably experienced some emotional stress just as He did to an even greater degree on the night of agony in the garden. He needed time alone to communicate with the Father and to assimilate this new revelation fully into His conscious awareness. He needed time in solitude to prepare spiritually for the day-to-day challenges that would face Him in His public ministry. There is a definite lesson to be learned in this example: We too should take time out for spiritual uplifting and preparation for the rigors of daily life. We should do this periodically during the year, as well as at the beginning of any major undertaking. The Lenten season provides us with just such an opportunity.

One means of spiritual uplifting which many people find most profitable is to think about or meditate on the life and actions of our Lord. The temptations experienced by our Lord while in the desert provide an opportunity for meditation from which we can gain some insight into our own life. This is particularly appropriate during the Lenten season.

Matthew and Luke both report three separate temptations. In the first, Jesus is hungry and is tempted to turn stones into bread. This is in a way similar to our own temptations to be overly concerned with material goods and the "easy life" when we should be concerned with our spiritual life.

Jesus is also tempted with power and dominion over the kingdoms of this world. Are we not also tempted many times to seek after power and personal glory in the business and social world of today, to work our way up the ladder, to be the one in charge and to direct others to do our will? Jesus gave us a definition of a real leader by showing us an example of one who came to serve *(cf. Jn 13:1-15; 21:15-17; Lk 22:24-27)*.

Finally, Jesus is tempted to throw himself off a high place to force a miracle which would show the power of God. How often have we of little faith demanded that God show us a sign? How often have we said, "If God would do such and such, I would believe"? Our Lord tells us in the parable of Lazarus and the rich man, "If they will not listen to Moses and the prophets, neither will they be persuaded if someone should rise from the dead" *(Lk 16:31)*. "Blessed are those who have not seen and have believed" *(Jn 20:29)*.

Yes, Jesus was truly tempted in the human nature that He shared with us, but He overcame His temptations and we, with His help, can do the same.

Recent years have witnessed a great revival of interest in the Bible among Catholics. With this renewed interest in the Scriptures it seems appropriate to introduce our young people to them so they can develop an appreciation and love for the Word of God. Merely telling them they should read the Bible is ineffective. A daily or even weekly Bible lesson can become tiring and lose its novelty after a while.

We think we have found a reasonable solution: When the Lenten season comes around, the children are generally looking for something to do for Lent. Quite often the emphasis is on *giving up* rather than on *doing something*. We have taken a positive approach by suggesting that we read one of the Gospels together during Lent. We started with the Gospel of Matthew and the following year it was Luke and then John. We read a chapter or a part of a chapter after supper each evening. The first year we just read and let it go at that but the following year we spent some time discussing and examining the meaning behind the words. We have obtained several Bible commentaries and the older children will often look up the explanation for certain passages themselves.

There are several good commentaries available. William Barkley's *Daily Study Bible* series on the New Testament is excellent in terms of cultural and historical background. We have used his books on both Luke and John and find new and vibrant life in the Word as he explains the background and meaning behind many of the passages. The Barkley series is published by the Westminster Press in Philadelphia. *The Jerome Biblical Commentary* (Prentice Hall) is an excellent one-volume commentary on the entire Bible and is recommended for understanding the Bible as it relates to Catholic doctrine. *A New Catholic Commentary On Holy Scripture* (Thomas Nelson) is another one-volume commentary we have found helpful. The latter two are expensive but do make a good investment that can be used for many years.

This Lenten practice is most beneficial for older (6th grade and up) children. For younger children simpler Bible stories may be preferable.

After completing the Gospels, we moved on to the Epistles. We concentrated on most of the Epistles of Paul in one year with the other Epistles receiving our attention the following year. Finally, we went through the Book of Revelation and then back to the Gospels for the benefit of the youngest. In this way, the children were exposed to most of the New Testament by the time they finished high school. They also were introduced to the Old Testament, since we went back and looked at many of the references we found in the Gospels.

Lest you think we may have forgotten the Book of Acts, I should mention that we encouraged the children to read this one on their own in preparation for confirmation. Acts is in many ways an adventure story and is more likely to hold their interest than any of the other books.

VIII
Holy Week / Easter Week

As we approach the end of Lent we come upon the most solemn and glorious time in the Church year. Our special mealtime celebrations begin on Holy Thursday. For the past several years our parish has had a special evening Mass to commemorate the Last Supper, which is followed by a covered dish supper in the church hall. We generally go as a family and join our fellow parishioners in the celebration of this special event.

In previous years we celebrated Holy Thursday at home in an altogether different manner. We reenacted the Last Supper at home after dinner on some evening during Holy Week. Obviously, Holy Thursday is the ideal time, but if more convenient, a day earlier in the week would serve as well.

The Last Supper was in fact a celebration of the Jewish feast of Passover, so we begin by a partial enactment of the Passover celebration. There are several books available that can lead you through it: The Archdiocese of Chicago, Liturgy Training Publications offers a small booklet entitled *The Passover Celebration*, edited by Rabbi Leon Klenicki, and *The Passover Meal* by Arleen Hynes is published by Paulist Press.

We have also used *The Passover Haggadah* (Shulsinger Brothers, 1960) in our celebration. This small booklet which tells the Passover story of the Exodus from Egypt is used in the Jewish Seder. In the interests of saving time we generally have not read the entire account but have picked parts which give us the general idea of the Passover celebration and its meaning. We then read one of the Gospel accounts of the Last Supper and the institution of the Eucharist. We reenact the Last Supper with unleavened bread and a cup of wine, which is passed around to all members of the family. The unleavened bread can be matzo from the supermarket or made at home by combining a half cup of warm water and a half cup of white flour with sufficient whole wheat flour (about one cup) to form a stiff dough with the right consistency for kneading. The dough should be kneaded thoroughly (at least five minutes) to avoid air pockets, and then covered with a damp towel and allowed to sit for five to ten minutes. The dough is then flattened and rolled out into an eight inch circle, placed on a cookie sheet or pizza pan and baked at 350 degrees for about fifteen minutes. The bread will break more easily if it is scored before baking.

As we act out the Last Supper, we explain to the children the parallel between the Passover of the Old Covenant and the New Passover of the New Covenant. The Jewish Passover recalls God's Covenant with His people and their passing over from bondage and slavery in Egypt to a new beginning in the Promised Land. In the New Covenant with Christ, we also "pass over" from the bondage and slavery of sin to a new life in Christ.

We also explain the connection between the Last Supper and the institution of the Eucharist; being careful, however, to point out to the children that our acting out is only that *acting out* and is not the same as the Eucharistic celebration of the Mass. In our reenactment, the bread and wine remain bread and wine; in the Mass there is a real change and as Jesus promised us, we receive His Body and Blood under the appearance of bread or wine.

Later in the evening of Holy Thursday we recall the suffering and agony of Jesus in the garden of Gethsemane and recall His words to the Apostles: "Could you not watch one hour with me?" *(Mt 26:40 Conf. Ed.)* We try to answer that question ourselves by spending some time praying in church that evening.

On Good Friday we again take part in the parish activities and substitute a special blessing for our evening grace before meals. The following blessing, given to us by Father Randal Gillette, C.P. is used on both Good Friday and Holy Saturday:

> *Heavenly Father, we praise You for having saved us*
> *through the suffering and death of Your Son.*
> *Forgive us our sins and lead us to greater dedication.*
> *Teach us to be obedient in faith,*
> *always ready to serve You by serving others in love.*
> *Bless this food and make us truly grateful for all the gifts*
> *You have shared with us through Christ our Lord. Amen.*

Easter is a glorious celebration which includes all the traditional festivities: Mass, holiday dinner, candy and colored eggs for the children.

For three years in a row we heard the Mass celebrant (a different priest each time) during his homily say, "We are Easter men and Alleluia is our song." This phrase made a lasting impression on the children, especially the youngest, so we incorporated it into our Easter grace before meals which we continue to use throughout Easter Week:

> *We are Easter people and Alleluia is our song.*
> *Let us join together and thank the Lord*
> *as we celebrate the Resurrection of His Son.*
> *We thank You Lord for our food upon the table*
> *We thank You for our family (and friends) to share it with*
> *But most of all we thank You for the glorious Resurrection of*
> *Your Son which we now celebrate.*
> ***Alleluia! Alleluia!***

IX

Pentecost

In recent years, there has been a renewed interest in the action of the third person of the Blessed Trinity, the Holy Spirit. Shortly before His death, Jesus promised to send the Holy Spirit to the Apostles (and to us). Judging by His words, He must have considered the coming of the Holy Spirit quite important. He said, "it is better for you that I go. For if I do not go, the Advocate will not come to you. But if I go, I will send him to you" *(Jn 16:7)*.

The feast of Pentecost commemorates the fulfillment of that promise and is one of the great feasts of the Church year. Pentecost has long been overshadowed by Christmas and Easter and probably always will be because of the secular additions to these holidays. We recall the importance of the Holy Spirit by emphasizing the significance of this feast in our family prayers.

The Christian celebration of Pentecost goes back at least to the second century and probably to the first century. Luke tells us that Paul "was hurrying to be in Jerusalem, if at all possible, for the day of Pentecost" *(Acts 20:16)*.

Our celebration of Pentecost is primarily a teaching and learning experience. We precede our Sunday dinner with some words from the Gospel of John *(Jn 16:5-7; 15:26; and 14:26)* and the following prayer:

Bless us, O Lord, and these Thy gifts,
which we are about to receive,
from thy bounty, through Christ our Lord
who promised us the gift of the Holy Spirit. Amen.

After dinner we read the first two chapters of the Acts of the Apostles. In discussing these readings we emphasize the importance that Jesus placed on the coming of the Holy Spirit and the remarkable transformation that took place in the Apostles.

As we read John 16:5-7 we realize that Jesus knew how much the Apostles relied on Him and yet He still could tell them that it was better for Him to go so that the Holy Spirit would come. Can you imagine anything better than having Jesus as your constant personal companion? But He said it would be better to have the Holy Spirit. Perhaps as we examine the transformation that took place in their lives we can begin to understand why He placed such great importance on the coming of the Holy Spirit.

There is ample evidence to indicate that even after three years of instruction the Apostles did not really understand His message *(cf. MT 26:56; Mk 8:31-33; 9:5-6, 10; 10:35-38; Jn 13:6-8; 14:5, 8-9)*. After the Crucifixion they were frightened and confused, and locked themselves in a room as they feared for their lives *(cf. Jn 20:19)*. Even after the Resurrection they still did not understand and still expected Jesus to be an earthly king of Israel *(cf. Acts 1:6)*.

Finally, the day of Pentecost came and these frightened, confused men who after three years of instruction still did not understand, were immediately and dramatically transformed by the Holy Spirit. They came out of hiding and began proclaiming the Word of God, which they now understood. Jesus had told them that the Spirit would instruct them in everything and remind them of all He had told them *(cf. Jn 14:26)*. That is exactly what happened and they were so overwhelmed that some of the observers thought they were drunk *(cf. Acts 2:12-13)*. The Holy Spirit had transformed them in such a way that they would never be the same again. They were enabled to go out into the whole world to preach the Good News of Jesus.

There is one additional point to be made as we celebrate Pentecost. This promise of transformation was not just for the Apostles. Luke tells us in Acts 1:14 that Mary and some other women were in their company and in Acts 2:4 we read that "they were all filled with the holy Spirit and began to speak in different tongues." Additionally, we read in Acts 11:15 the words of Peter (referring to the household of the Gentile, Cornelius) "the holy Spirit fell upon them as it had upon us at the beginning."

There is much more to be said about the action of the Holy Spirit in our own lives, but we save that for a later time, when we dedicate the entire month of September to the Holy Spirit.

X

March

The Month of Saint Joseph

Marchninineteenth has long been the special day on which we remember and honor Saint Joseph, the foster father of Jesus. It is also traditional to set aside the entire month of March in honor of Saint Joseph. We use the month of March as an opportunity to present an introductory teaching on the saints in order to give our children a deeper understanding of the Communion of Saints and our interdependence through Christian prayer.

The early Christians used the term *saint* to refer to all the faithful, whether living on earth or in the next world. They considered themselves all to be part of one *People of God* that would someday be reunited in Heaven. Over the years, the term began to be applied primarily to those members of the People of God who were in Heaven and more specifically to those who after an exhaustive Church investigation were determined most likely to be in Heaven.

The fact that a deceased loved one has not been proclaimed a saint in no way indicates that he or she is not in Heaven. In fact, the Church acknowledges that there are many in Heaven who will never be proclaimed saints. These are part of what the Church calls the Church Triumphant, while we here on earth who are still working out our salvation are called the Church Militant. The Roman Church designates a special day to honor all the Church Triumphant. This feast (celebrated at least as early as the fourth century) is called All Saints Day and has been celebrated on the first of November since the ninth century.

But, what does it really mean to be designated a saint?

First, it means that some group of people, usually a religious order, has found cause to remember and honor the memory of a deceased loved one. The group promotes the memory of the deceased and requests an official investigation of the person's life and writings. They ask in their prayers that the deceased intercede for them in their needs. A record of all favors received through this intercession is kept and forwarded to the investigating commission. After a thorough investigation of the person's life and after some authentic favors or cures (miracles) have been attributed to the deceased, he or she will be declared *blessed.* To be declared blessed simply means that it is likely the deceased is a member of the Church Triumphant in Heaven. After additional investigation and favors or cures the person can finally be officially proclaimed a saint. Being proclaimed a saint then means that as far as can be determined by human earthly means, we believe the person is truly a member of the Church Triumphant.

But, why should we honor the saints?

Paul, in his letters to the Corinthians, Philippians and Thessalonians says, "be imitators of me" *(1 Cor 4:16; cf. Phil 3:17; 2 Thes 3:7).* We do this in the secular world when we hold up national heroes like George Washington and Abraham Lincoln. We give these men and many others a special day of commemoration and tell our youth to imitate their virtues. If we are concerned with our salvation, is it not also appropriate to imitate those the Church holds up as good and faithful people? What better way to remember these holy people than to go to church and praise God in their honor and memory? Thus it is that the Church designates specific days for certain saints to be remembered at the Eucharistic celebration. When we read of their lives and struggles, it can be a great source of inspiration to us on our own way to glory.

But, what about intercession, or the prayers of the saints?

Let us first consider this question as it applies to the Church Militant, or the living *saints* as the word was used in the early centuries. Asking another member of the Body of Christ to pray for us in no way negates the fact that there is "one mediator between God and the human race, Christ Jesus" *(1 Tim 2:5)*. All things are accomplished in and through Jesus and "without him nothing came to be" *(Jn 1:3)*. There is however, a strong tradition from the early Church which points to the acceptance and desirability of praying for one another.

We know fully that Jesus Christ is our only mediator of justice. Through His merits alone we have been reconciled with God and it is through Him alone that we obtain our salvation. We know equally well that God has made us a community people and given us an interdependence of grace when He tells us to "love one another as I love you" *(Jn 15:12)*. One of the ways in which Jesus loved us was to pray for His disciples *(cf. Jn 17:9)* and for all believers *(cf. Jn 17:20)* and even for those who put Him to death *(cf. Lk 23:34)*. In Luke's Gospel we find that Jesus prayed for Peter and told him that he in turn must strengthen his brothers *(cf. Lk 22:32)*. This strengthening most certainly would have included Peter's own prayers for his brothers.

This idea of interdependence (through prayer) is a strong theme in the teaching of Paul and is evident in almost every letter he writes. Paul constantly exhorts the faithful to pray for each other; he often speaks of his prayers for them and he even invites (or perhaps urges) them to share in his own ministry through prayers offered on his behalf *(cf. Rom 15:30-32; 1 Cor 1:4; 2 Cor 1:8-11; Eph 6:18-20; 2 Thes 1:11; 3:1-3; 1 Tim 2:1; 2 Tim 1:3; Phlm 1:22)*.

In the Book of Acts we find reference to the extraordinary miracles "God accomplished at the hands of Paul" *(Acts 19:11)*. Verse 12 even extends this power to handkerchiefs or cloths which had touched Paul's skin. We must be careful not to become superstitious and attribute this power to the instrument itself, but rather to the power of God made present to us through another person or a material symbol.

The letters of James and John as well as the letter to the Hebrews also exhort us to pray for one another *(cf. Jas 5:16; 1 Jn 5:14-16; Heb 13:18)*. In the Book of Acts we find the example of Stephen, the first martyr, praying for his persecutors *(cf. Acts 7:60)*. That prayer was answered in the person of Saint Paul, who participated in Stephen's persecution but later became a great Apostle for the Lord.

Inasmuch as the early Church considered the members of the Church Militant and the Church Triumphant all members of the one Body of Christ, it would seem natural for the Church Militant to expect the Church Triumphant to remember them when they came to glory. Scripture tells us explicitly that the angels are aware of what happens here on earth, and that they also intercede physically to aid us in our hour of need *(cf. Lk 15:10; Jn 20:12; Acts 12:7; 27:23-24; Heb 1:14)*. Early tradition assumes the same of the Church Triumphant. The letter to the Hebrews reminds us that we are surrounded by a great cloud of heavenly witnesses *(cf. Heb 12:1)*. And the Book of Maccabees *(cf. 2 Macc 15:14)* tells us that the Prophet Jeremiah prays in Heaven for his people and their holy city.

This tradition may well have developed further during the time of persecution. Early Christians who had been condemned to death for the faith (martyrdom) did not look on their fate with fear but rather with joy and anticipation. They would soon be face-to-face with God. Would it not seem natural for a close friend or relative to ask that they be remembered when the martyr entered the fullness of the Kingdom of God? And so there developed the idea and tradition of a close bond between the Church Militant and the Church Triumphant. The Church has traditionally referred to this bond as the *Communion of Saints.*

Saint Jerome provides a concise summary of early Church thought in *Contra Vigilantium* written in the year 406.

There was in western Gaul an early Christian priest named Vigilantius who had attacked the veneration of saints and relics. It was against the teachings of Vigilantius that Saint Jerome wrote his pointed treatise. He defends the long tradition of honor paid to relics, but clearly states that we do not adore the martyrs. We simply honor them in worship of Him whose martyrs they are. He further defends the notion of the Communion of Saints when he writes, "If Apostles and martyrs while still in the body can pray for others, when they ought still to be anxious for themselves, how much more must they do so when they have won their crowns, overcome and triumphed? Moses wins pardon from God; and Stephen, the first Christian martyr, entreats pardon for his persecutors; once they have entered on their life with Christ, shall they have less power than before?"

The Church does not command but strongly encourages devotion to and imitation of these special members of the Body of Christ in the Church Triumphant.

It is as part of this encouragement that the month of March is dedicated to Saint Joseph, the foster father of Jesus and also the special patron of the Universal Church.

Saint Joseph has many qualities worthy of consideration and imitation. He was a simple working man, a carpenter, and as Matthew tells us "a righteous man" *(Mt 1:19)*. Matthew portrays Joseph as a man of great faith who puts his trust in the Lord *(cf. Mt 1:20-25; 2:13-14; 2:19-21)*. There is little else that is known for certain about Joseph, but one thing is obvious: God specifically chose him for a very special position and he responded unhesitantly. The Litany of Saint Joseph which includes many of the virtues of this faithful servant provides us with a teaching tool as we explain the need for these virtues in ourselves and our children.

As our family observance of the Month of Saint Joseph we discuss the Communion of Saints and our relationship to those faithful who have gone before us. We also add a simple prayer to the end of our grace before meals: "Saint Joseph, protector of the Holy Family and patron of the Universal Church, pray for us." Thus our mealtime blessing becomes:

> *Bless us, O Lord, and these Thy gifts,*
> *which we are about to receive, from Thy bounty,*
> *through Christ our Lord. Amen.*
> *Saint Joseph, protector of the Holy Family and*
> *patron of the Universal Church, pray for us. Amen.*

The Litany of the Saints is also appropriate for an after-meal prayer sometime during the month of March, but we must carefully monitor the reaction of our children and gage their attention span. It is important to avoid making our mealtime prayer into a burdensome exercise. Prayer should spring from the heart in a natural and spontaneous response to our loving God. If our zeal overflows into a burdensome experience, our children will not easily develop that loving, prayerful relationship with the Lord which we seek through our mealtime prayer and catechesis.

XI

April

Month of the Holy Eucharist

Although the Eucharist is the center of the Church's worship, it is often not fully understood. During April, the month of the Holy Eucharist, we try to give our children a greater understanding and appreciation of the Eucharist and the Mass.

In the Mass, we find a number of external signs which remind us of the presence of Jesus: We gather in His Name and share His Word in Holy Scripture. We are reminded of His public ministry as we listen to the Gospel and we recall the Last Supper as we hear the words of consecration. These external signs make up what is sometimes referred to as the *sign value* of the Mass. We have used the following illustration as an aid to understanding the sign value of the Eucharistic celebration and the background and origins of this wonderful sacrament.

Picture in your mind a man who has been unemployed for some time, who now has an opportunity for a high paying job. It will mean much to his family. Bills can be paid, they can partake more abundantly of the material necessities of life; perhaps a college education is now possible for the children. But there is a problem: the job is in a remote area of the world. He will have to be away for a number of years while his wife and children remain behind. Plans have been in the works for several weeks and now the time of departure is only hours away. It's a beautiful Sunday morning. The family goes to church together and returns home for Sunday dinner. Close friends and relatives have joined the family and a special meal has been prepared. As they gather around the table they are particularly thankful for this opportunity to come together and share a meal. There is, however, a note of sadness brought on by the man's impending departure. He leads them in prayer and then pours some wine, lifts his glass and proposes a toast to their love for one another. He declares that mere physical separation cannot destroy the love they have and reminds them that he will return one day and they will be together again. He knows that as a loving father and head of the household, he has exerted a strong influence and has been a stabilizing factor in the family. He is concerned about the difficulties his wife will have in raising the children without his firm support. He wants the older children to remember him and the younger ones to come to know him in his absence.

What can he do to stabilize the family while he is far away? Certainly he will write letters to his wife and she can share some of the news with the children. He may even write an occasional letter directly to the children. But he feels the need for more. As this last Sunday dinner comes to a close, he pauses and looks around the table at his wife and children. He tells them he is thankful for this time they have spent together and that they will always be with him in his heart. He tells them they should not dwell on his departure, but rather think of the time when he will return and they will be together again. He reminds them that in the long run it is really better that he go. The mother tells the children, as she wipes a tear from her own eye, that it is really Daddy who is making a sacrifice and will have a harder time. They will still have each other, but he will be alone in a foreign country. They turn and look at him and then he says, "I want you to love one another as I have loved you and I want you to help each other."

Turning to the older children he adds, "And I want you especially to help your mother in my absence and set a good example for your brothers and sisters. And there is one more thing I want you to do while I am away. Each Sunday after church I want you to share a meal together as a family and remember that I will be thinking of you. In this way we will all be together in spirit. One of you can pour some wine and propose a toast to the mutual love and unity of our family, as I have done today. Perhaps as the younger children get older you can tell them stories of the times we spent together and our plans for the future. In this way our family can remain strong and unified until I return and we can be together again."

The preceding illustration is not so different, from what Jesus did for us at the Last Supper. He told us, "It is better for you that I go" (Jn 16:7). He said "I have eagerly desired to eat this Passover with you before I suffer" (Lk 22:15). He took bread, blessed it, and gave it to them saying, "This is my body, which will be given for you" (Lk 22:19). He blessed the wine and said, "This cup is the new convenant in my blood, which will be shed for you" (Lk 22:20). And He said "do this in memory of me" (Lk 22:19).

Paul tells us in his first letter to the Corinthians, "For as often as you eat this bread and drink the cup, you proclaim the death of the Lord until He comes" (1 Cor 11:26). We see, then, that Jesus gave us a way to remember Him and a sign of His presence and His saving actions.

While the preceding illustration can give us some appreciation of the sign value of the Mass, the Eucharist is much more than just a sign of His presence; He is really and truly present among us. It is this belief in the true presence as well as the ideas of sacrifice and celebration that we try to impart to our children during our April discussions.

The Mass has traditionally been called the *Sacrifice of the Mass*. The source of this tradition reaches back at least to the latter part of the Apostolic era. Space does not permit a complete discussion of this tradition, but I think a brief outline will help to better understand the sacrificial aspect of the Mass.

Let us first review the background from which it came, that is, the Jewish ritual of sacrifice under the Old Covenant. It was important for the Jews, through the hands of their priests, to make a sacrifice to God. This was particularly true at Passover time, when the Jews would sacrifice the paschal lamb and then eat the Passover meal as they recalled their deliverance from bondage in Egypt to freedom in the Promised Land. In the New Covenant Jesus Himself becomes both priest and victim, as the *Lamb of God*. He offers Himself on the Cross in satisfaction for our sins. He gives us a New Covenant in which we pass over from the bondage of sin to the freedom of new life. He tells us the bread is His Body, which is to be given up for us, and the cup is His Blood, which is to be shed for us. He commands us then to remember His death and Resurrection as He says, "do this in memory of me" *(Lk 22:19)*.

As the early Church Fathers reflected on the relationship between the bread and cup of the Last Supper and the sacrifice on Calvary, they began to realize the true significance of what Jesus had left them (and us). They realized how the Eucharist of the New Covenant replaced the paschal lamb of the Old Covenant, so that we have a true sacrifice in which we give honor and glory to God by our participation.

For a fuller understanding of the sacrificial aspects of the Eucharist I recommend Raymond Brown's book *Priest and Bishop* (Paulist Press, 1970) and *The Meaning of the Sacraments* (Pflaum/Standard, 1972) by Monika Hellwig.

In recent years there has been a much greater emphasis on the Mass as a celebration.

The Mass brings the *New Israel*, the new *People of God* together to recall the death and Resurrection of our Lord and Savior. It should be a wondrous and joyous occasion as we rejoice in Christ our Savior who has redeemed us and given us the promise of eternal life.

Finally, in our consideration of the Eucharist, we discuss the real presence of Jesus. In years past the term *transubstantiation* was used and explained very technically in terms of Greek philosophy. We mention and explain transubstantiation briefly, but prefer to rely on faith in Jesus and His Word for our belief in the real presence.

We recall two stories from the Gospels which demonstrate the power that Jesus exercised over His body and over ordinary bread. The first story shows Jesus with complete authority over His physical body, defying the laws of nature as He walks across the water *(cf. Mt 14:22-33; Mk 6:45-52; Jn 6:16-24)*. The second story shows the authority which Jesus exercised over bread, when He fed 5,000 people with only five loaves of bread *(cf. Mt 14:13-21; Mk 6:34-44; Lk 9:10-17; Jn 6:1-15)*.

Later in the Gospels, we read that Jesus took bread and said "this is my body" and He took wine and said "this is my blood" *(cf. Mt 26:26-28; Mk 14:22-24; Lk 22:19-20)* and we believe because it is His Word.

In order to emphasize the uniqueness of His presence in the Eucharist, we discuss several different ways in which Jesus is present in one place at the same time. First of all, Jesus is present everywhere, because He is God and God is omnipresent. Secondly, He told us that where two or three are gathered in His Name He is there in their midst *(cf. Mt 18:20)*. Now, you may say, "Of course He's there, He's everywhere." But it seems reasonable to me that He must be there in a *different* way where two or three are gathered in His Name. Otherwise, He would not have made a special point of it.

We have now seen two different ways in which Jesus is present in the same place at the same time. If we consider the Mystical Body of Christ, we find another way in which Jesus is present among us in the same place at the same time but in a different manner. Jesus is also present to us in His Word in Holy Scripture. In the second chapter of his book *Where is your god?* (Geo. A Pflaum, 1966) Donald Gray discusses ways of being present and offers additional insight for those interested in further reading.

The Eucharist is another totally different and distinct way in which Jesus becomes present among us. This real presence of Jesus under the appearance of bread and wine is a mystery we cannot fully understand (even with the philosophical explanation of transubstantiation).

There are many excellent books that try to theologize and explain the presence of Jesus in the Eucharist; but I must confess that after having read several of them, I still come back to the simple statement that Jesus is really present in the "bread of life" *(Jn 6:48)* which He gave us to nourish our spiritual life because He said so. He said, "whoever eats this bread will live forever" *(Jn 6:51)*.

In our mealtime prayer for April, we offer a thanksgiving for the food that nourishes our physical life and the *Bread of Life* that nourishes our spiritual life:

LEADER: *Lord Jesus you taught us to say:*

ALL: *Give us this day our daily bread.*

LEADER: *As we thank You for the daily bread which we are about to partake for our physical life we are mindful also of Your gift of daily bread for our spiritual life.*

ALL: *For our daily bread we thank You Lord Jesus.*

We have also used the traditional mealtime blessing with a simple reference to the Bread of Life as follows:

Bless us, O Lord, and these Thy gifts,
which we are about to receive,
from Thy bounty, through Christ our Lord
who gives us our Eucharistic **Bread of Life.**
Amen.

XII

May

The Month of Mary

For most Catholics, May has always been Mary's month. Indeed, Mary's month of May is the oldest and best known of all the month-long devotional designations. Many people can recall from childhood fond memories of May crownings and processions or other special May devotions. May is a beautiful month, the sun warms the earth, the flowers burst into bloom and a special relationship with the Mother of God warms the heart and fills us with the joy of her Son, Jesus Christ.

Some will ask, why so much fuss over Mary? Why this special love for Mary? I would answer that question with another question: Why does a child have a special love for its mother?

Jesus Christ alone is our Savior who has redeemed us from our sins through His Precious Blood on the Cross; but in God's plan for our salvation He has deigned to give us Mary to be our spiritual mother. As our heavenly mother, Mary loves and cares for us in the spiritual realm even more than our earthly mothers do in the temporal realm.

In the very first recorded instance of God's revelation of His plan for our salvation we find the place of *the woman* as God says to the serpent in the Garden of Eden "I will put enmity between you and the woman, and between your off-spring and hers" *(Gen 3:15)*. The prophet Isaiah tells us some 700 years before the birth of Christ that the Messiah was to be born of a woman *(cf. Is 7:14)*.

God was free to choose His plan of salvation according to His divine will, and He chose to make His plan depen-dent on the free will cooperation of a woman, a human being who like us was free to accept or reject God's plan. God in effect put His whole plan in jeopardy, subject to the acceptance or rejection of His maidservant Mary. He sent the Angel Gabriel to ask Mary's cooperation and participa-tion in His plan for our salvation. Mary, in her faith and love for God, replied "I am the handmaid of the Lord. May it be done to me according to your word" *(Lk 1:38)*. It was at that moment, after Mary's free acceptance, that "the Word became flesh and made his dwelling among us" *(Jn 1:14)*. It was at that moment, when Mary humbly agreed to partici-pate in God's plan, that she first became the spiritual moth-er of the whole human race destined to be saved through the merits of her Son, our Lord, Jesus Christ.

Mary also showed herself to be our mother as she stood in sorrow and agony at the foot of the Cross and offered her Son on our behalf. Mary can truly be said to have offered her Son; Pontius Pilate openly declared that he found no guilt in Jesus and certainly Mary could have appeared before Pilate to plead on behalf of her Son thereby obtaining His release. Mary chose instead to suffer with her Son, as the prophet Simeon had fore-told when he said, "thy own soul a sword shall pierce" *(Lk 2:35 Conf. Ed.)*. Anyone who doubts the suffering of Mary should think first of a mother's grief at the loss of a son and then consider, that this mother was compelled to stand for several hours and literally watch her Son die.

That Mary is our mother was also confirmed by our Lord Himself as He hung on the Cross and said to His mother

"Woman, behold, your son" *(Jn 19:26)* referring directly to the disciple John and indirectly to the whole human race as represented by John. He also turned to John and said "Behold, your mother" *(Jn 19:27)*.

She is truly our mother and it is for that reason that we love her and have recourse to her.

In an earlier chapter, we discussed the desirability of imitating the virtues of the saints. In this regard Mary can do much for us. Mary's faith in God was total; she trusted in the Lord completely. The Annunciation *(cf. Lk 1:26-38)*, the flight into Egypt and the return *(cf. Mt 2:13-14, 19-22)*, the marriage feast at Cana *(cf. Jn 2:1-12)* and Mary's vigil at the foot of the Cross *(cf. Jn 19:25)* all attest to her undying faith. Her humility is also worthy of consideration: She was troubled when the angel called her blessed among women *(cf. Lk 1:29)*, she called herself the servant of the Lord *(cf. Lk 1:38, 48)*, and when Elizabeth praised her, Mary immediately proclaimed the greatness of the Lord and her own lowliness *(cf. Lk 1:45-55)*. Mary has also given us a fine example of love and charity towards others in her visitation to Elizabeth *(cf. Lk 1:39-56)*.

Many times God used other beings, both angels and men, as instruments to dispense His grace and lead His people. He is always able to intervene directly and communicate His will and His grace personally, but for some reason known only to Him, He often chooses to work through others. Holy Scripture, God's own Word, abounds with examples of God dispensing His grace through the hands of others. The Book of Exodus records the actions of Moses as God's instrument in leading His people out of bondage. Chapter 16 in the first Book of Samuel records how the Lord sent Samuel to anoint David. The Book of Tobit contains a fascinating story of God using one of His creatures (the Angel Raphael) to lead and cure on His behalf. In the New Testament we find the Angel Gabriel announcing God's message *(cf. Lk 1:26-37)* and an angel of the Lord freeing Peter from his chains in response to the prayers of the community (cf. Acts 12:4-14). Numerous miraculous cures at the hands of the Apostles are also recorded. Acts 3 tells us that in the Name of Jesus, Peter cured a man crippled from birth; in Acts 5:16, we find that the people would bring their sick to the Apostles and all were cured. And in Acts 19:12, it is recorded that even cloths which had touched the skin of Paul brought about miraculous cures.

God has also used Mary as an instrument to dispense His grace. The first two miracles that Jesus performed were wrought through the action of Mary. Luke records the first miracle of grace when he tells us that Elizabeth was filled with the Holy Spirit and the babe in her womb leapt at Mary's greeting (cf. Lk 1:41). Jesus' first miracle in the physical order was also performed at Mary's request. John has left us a vivid record of Mary's concern for others and her faith in the power of God as well as her intercessory powers in the story of the marriage at Cana (cf. Jn 2:1-11).

Jesus chose Mary as His means of coming to us. Many saints throughout history have proclaimed that there is no better way, no quicker way, no more perfect means to go to Jesus Christ than through the same channel which He chose in coming to us. If you would have Jesus come into your life, you would do well to ask Mary to bring Him; to present Him mystically in the temple of our hearts as she presented Him physically in the Jewish Temple.

We look to the person of Pope John Paul II, to find a living example of this truth. John Paul, following the teaching of Saint Louis de Montfort's *True Devotion to Mary*, long ago consecrated himself to Jesus through Mary and continues tirelessly to serve Jesus in union with Mary.

During the month of May, we try to give our children a greater understanding of Mary's place in God's plan of salvation. We look at the words of Luke in the first two chapters of the third Gospel. We look at Luke 1:38 and consider Mary's free choice to participate in God's plan. We listen to Elizabeth's praise of Mary (cf. Lk 1:42) and ponder Mary's humble response in the Magnificat (cf. Lk 1:46-55). Finally,

Simeon's prophecy *(cf. Lk 2:35)* foretells Mary's participation in Jesus' redemptive acts.

We also look to the Gospel of John for another picture of Mary's presence in God's saving plan. But to see the message of Mary's participation in the fourth Gospel requires some background knowledge and understanding of the way John writes.

John always has an underlying and sometimes subtle message. His choice of stories, the setting, and the very order and arrangement quite often tell a story of their own. In examining Mary's connection with the mission of Jesus, we are primarily interested in two stories that take place at the very beginning and the very end of Jesus' ministry: the wedding feast at Cana and the Crucifixion. John places Mary in both of these stories, thereby showing her to be a full participant from beginning to end.

Within these stories in the Gospel of John we can find in capsule form a complete course in Mariology.

In the Cana story, we find first an example of Mary's profound awareness and concern for the needs of others. Then we see Mary's automatic response as she turns immediately to her Son for a solution to the problem. This incident is especially interesting when you consider that Jesus, who was always aware of the happenings around Him, must have known that the wine had run out. And yet, John tells us that it was Mary who became concerned and Mary who brought that concern to Jesus. The response of Jesus and the use of the words "hour" and "woman" are of more than mere historical importance.

The hour referred to in the Cana story is the hour of salvation which we find fulfilled in the Crucifixion story. The significance is that it is only through the grace of God and the glory of Jesus Christ (which is brought about in the "hour" of sacrifice on the Cross) that Mary assumes her full place in the economy of salvation. At Cana, that hour when Jesus would confirm her place as the spiritual mother of the Church and all mankind had not yet arrived. In spite of the fact that the hour has not yet come, we see that Jesus will not refuse His mother. He grants her request in anticipation of that hour in which He will exalt her to the position she now holds through the grace of God.

Mary's faith in both the ability and the willingness of Jesus is overwhelmingly evident in this story. Mary does not ask Jesus again, she does not plead with Him; she simply assumes what she knows to be true, that Jesus will not refuse. Even though He has in effect said no, she proceeds confidently and says to the steward "Do whatever he tells you" (Jn 2:5).

Jesus' response is immediate and complete, as He performs this first physical miracle at the request of His mother.

John's use of the word "woman" in both the Cana story and the Crucifixion story is equally significant. This unusual form of address to a mother by her Son is seen by many as a direct reference to the *woman* in Genesis 3:15. One of the earliest titles of Mary is "the New Eve." It was in this title that the early Fathers of the Church saw Mary's role in rectifying the fault of the *first* Eve. The New Eve, Mary, is the true (spiritual) mother of the human race.

Another reference to the *woman* is found in the Book of Jeremiah (cf. Jer 31:22) in what the *New Catholic Commentary* calls "the most mysterious and difficult text of the entire book." So hidden, in fact, is the meaning of this passage that a review of several versions of the Book of Jeremiah reveals a variety of strange translations. The most likely literal translation of the Hebrew is "woman surrounds man." The Douay Version thus renders it ". . . a woman shall compass a man;" while the New American Bible offers ". . . the woman must encompass the man" and then adds the words "with devotion" which the footnote clearly states are not in the Hebrew but have been "added for the sense." Monsignor Ronald Knox in his translation of the Latin Vulgate gives us ". . . weak woman is to be the protectress of man's strength," while the Jerusalem Bible offers ". . . the Woman sets out to find her Husband again." The Revised Standard Version has ". . . a woman protects a man."

The commentaries and interpretations seem to be at least as numerous and varied as the translations. While there is disagreement among scholars on the exact meaning of this passage, all is not lost. The long-standing tradition of the Church as found in the writings and teachings of many of the saints offers us some enlightenment; and Saint Alphonsus Liguori, in his book *The Glories of Mary* (TAN, 1977), presents without hesitation or question, the meaning of this passage: The Word of God through the prophet Jeremiah is referring first to the Incarnation of the Eternal Word in the womb of Mary His mother and then to the continuing mystery of Mary's spiritual maternity. Jesus Christ is the center and source of all grace, but inasmuch as *the woman encompasses the man* that grace which comes from Jesus, must also pass through the hands of Mary, just as a line drawn from the center of a circle must pass through the circumference of that circle.

We find then in this obscure passage of Jeremiah (i.e. "The LORD has created a new thing upon the earth: the woman must encompass the man" (*Jer 31:22*)) a summary of the teachings of Saint Alphonsus Liguori and Saint Louis de Montfort which they in turn have gleaned from the writings of a long list of other saints, scholars and mystics. This list includes, but is not limited to St. Augustine, St. John Chrysostom, St. Ephrem, St. Cyril, St. Germanus, St. John Damascene, St. Anselm, St. Bernadine, St. Thomas Aquinas, St. Bridget and St. Bonaventure.

The teaching is simply this: God alone is all powerful and the Author of all grace and was totally free to choose His own plan for dispensing that grace. He had no need for any other agent; He did not have any absolute need for Mary, since she is, in comparison with the Most High, as nothing, for he alone is *He Who Is*. In fact, He did not even have to send His only Son into the world. God was completely free to choose His plan, and He did. God created a new thing upon the earth *(cf. Jer 31:22)*: God sent His only Son into the world to be our source of grace, and He deemed that the woman would encompass the man so that His grace would flow to us through her. In God's plan He gave us a Brother and a Mother to foster and nurture our spiritual life. All we have to do is turn to them and ask and we shall receive.

In the Month of May we turn our thoughts to our mother Mary and as we gather to say our grace before the evening meal we include one decade of the Scriptural Rosary. We say the Lord's Prayer (the Our Father) and then read the ten scripture verses followed by a single Angelic Salutation (the Hail Mary) and a Glory be to the Father. The October chapter contains a more complete description of the Rosary and our use of it at mealtimes during the months of May and October.

XIII

June

Month of the Sacred Heart of Jesus

Devotion to the Sacred Heart of Jesus has become one of the most popular and well-known practices of piety within the Roman Catholic Church. In large part, this is due to the widespread publication of private revelations made to Saint Margaret Mary Alacoque in the French town of Paray-le-Monial in the late sixteen hundreds. In fact, the revelations and the devotion are so closely related that the revelations are popularly assumed to be the actual source of the devotion to the Sacred Heart of Jesus.

Actually, the basis for devotion to the Heart of Jesus and to the Precious Blood which flowed from it can be traced back to Calvary and the very beginnings of Christianity.

In the prophet Isaiah we read:

"I will pour out water upon the thirsty ground,
and streams upon the dry land;
I will pour out my spirit upon your offspring,
and my blessings upon your descendants." *(Is 44:3)*

And in John's Gospel we find that Jesus said from within Him would come forth rivers of living water (cf. Jn 4:10-14; 7:38). The Gospel of John further tells us that a "soldier thrust his lance into his side, and immediately blood and water flowed out" (Jn 19:34). This pouring forth of blood and water is interpreted in early Patristic teaching as an outpouring of the Spirit upon the infant Church. The source of this blood and water flowing from the Savior's side (and thus the Spirit which was poured out upon the Church) was the very Heart of Christ. Pierre Barbet in his book A Doctor at Calvary presents medical opinion and evidence which confirms that the lance did in fact pierce the Heart of Jesus.

The human heart has always been symbolically associated with human emotions such as love, compassion and sorrow; a person's whole inner being with all its strengths and weaknesses, is often symbolized by the heart. Thus, we say he has a strong heart, a wicked heart, a generous heart, a repentant heart, a brave heart or perhaps, he has no heart, meaning lack of courage or lack of compassion depending on the context.

Holy Scripture abounds in this metaphorical reference to the human heart. We also find similar references to the heart of God (cf. Gen 6:6; 1 Sam 13:14; Jer 30:24; Jer 31:20).

Jesus, being both God and man would combine within His person both the human and divine qualities of the heart. It is particularly the love of the Heart of Jesus that is found through devotion to the Sacred Heart. The physical human Heart of Jesus symbolically represents both the human and divine love and mercy that Jesus manifests for all mankind. The early Church saw this love from the Heart of Jesus as the source of the "living water" referred to by Jesus in John's Gospel and Isaiah's prophecy.

Throughout the Patristic writings of the early Church, we find numerous references to the wounded side of Jesus. They speak often of the Spirit which flowed from that wound to sustain the early Church. The fourth century historian Eusebius of Caesarea has preserved a letter which tells of the deacon, Sanctus, a martyr in the year 177, who was strengthened by this living water flowing from the Savior.

Although the basis for devotion to the Heart of Jesus goes back to Apostolic times, there does not seem to be any significant or widespread practice of this devotion during the first ten centuries. The early writers concentrated most often on the external wound and the Spirit flowing from it. Only later, and on rare occasions, do we find mention of the Sacred Heart, as some of the spiritual mystics found their way through the wounded side to the source of the Spirit and love of Christ.

It is not until the eleventh or twelfth centuries that we witness the strong beginnings of a spiritual awareness and development of a devotion whose object is the wounded Heart of the Savior. During this time, the devotion became rather widespread among the Benedictine and Cistercian monasteries, but remained a totally private devotion of individual, fervent souls.

The first indication of the devotion's future importance comes towards the very end of the thirteenth century in the form of a vision granted to Saint Gertrude (d. 1302) on the feast of Saint John the Evangelist. In the vision she rested her head near the wound in the Savior's side and heard the beating of the Divine Heart. She asked John if he had felt this delightful heartbeat on the night of the Last Supper, and why he had never spoken of it. John replied that this revelation had been saved for a later time when the world, having grown cold, would need it to rekindle its love. That this vision and these words were indeed prophetic has been confirmed by subsequent history.

The several hundred years up to and through the sixteenth century saw the continued spread of this devotion and the formulating of prayers and special exercises. But still it remained primarily an individual and private devotion practiced by a relatively small number of people.

In the first half of the seventeenth century, there began a movement known as Jansenism, named after its chief initiator Cornelius Jansen. This movement attempted to stay within the framework of the Catholic Church but wanted to alter some of the teachings and administrative details of the Church. The background and context of the Jansenist ideas are too complex to be adequately discussed in this work. However, the principle points of Jansenism centered around the fallen human nature and total unworthiness of the person, contrasted with the awesome unreachableness and majesty of God, the Creator and Judge.

The situation was rendered even more complex when the Jansenist movement joined forces with other groups which fed on nationalistic and anti-papal sentiments caused at least in part by the conflicting temporal and spiritual powers of the Holy See. The best known of these nationalistic movements within the Church was the Gallicans in France, who attempted to make the French Church almost totally independent of Rome.

As a result of Jansenism's overemphasis on the unworthiness of mankind, the gulf between God and man developed into an uncrossable abyss, in sharp contrast to the words of Jesus who taught us to call God "Father" or "Abba" which is rendered as the familiar "daddy" of a child. As the errors of the Jansenists gained widespread acceptance among both the clergy and the laity, the spirituality of the people waned and grew cold. Jansenism was a *dogma of despair* and the people became indifferent and turned away from the Lord. This was perhaps most evident in the infrequent reception of the sacraments.

It was for this time of spiritual emptiness that Divine Providence had reserved the fullness of the devotion to the Sacred Heart of Jesus. It was to fulfill the great need for a spiritual renewal that this devotion began to be fully manifested. After centuries of smoldering, the flame of love in the Heart of Jesus was ready to burst into the world.

In 1670, St. John Eudes celebrated a feast of the Heart of Jesus in what was the first truly public manifestation of this devotion. The prophetic words of Saint Gertrude's vision of almost four centuries earlier were about to be fulfilled. However, it would still be another two centuries before the Sacred Heart of Jesus would enflame and renew the entire Catholic Church. And it would not be until the nineteenth century that we would finally see the end of the Jansenist errors.

Although there were others before her, it was Saint Margaret Mary Alacoque to whom our Lord chose to reveal His wishes in great detail. This revelation took place over a period of years, from 1673 until 1675, and provided the basis for the widespread and popular devotion to the Sacred Heart which has been so evident in this century.

The public spread of devotion to the Sacred Heart was slow and difficult at first; there was strong opposition from the Jansenists to both the devotion and the Jesuits who were attempting to foster spiritual renewal through the Heart of Jesus. In the face of ongoing resistance, the movement continued to make slow and steady progress, so that by 1726, there were more than 300 Sacred Heart associations. The devotion was known throughout Europe and had been introduced in the Far East and the Americas. By 1765, there were 700 new confraternities and when Pius IX extended the feast of the Sacred Heart to the entire Church in 1856 he was only confirming what already existed. Almost every diocese in the world had previously secured the privilege of a special feast in honor of the Sacred Heart. By the middle of the nineteenth century, the Jansenist errors had been eliminated and the Heart of Jesus reigned over the hearts of the faithful throughout the Catholic Church.

The proper object of this devotion is the human and divine love which Jesus manifests for each person individually. The constant theme of our Lord's message to Saint Margaret Mary was one of overwhelming love and His desire for the happiness and well-being of all people. His great lament was that "This Heart which has so loved men has received only rejection and indifference in return." The Heart of Jesus is enflamed with love for us and He asks that we come to Him, that we might have eternal happiness.

In his first letter, John tells us that "the Son of God was revealed to destroy the works of the devil" *(1 Jn 3:8)* and it is for this same reason that He has revealed the love of His Sacred Heart. Jesus desires to bring us unto Himself, that we might live in Him and He in us *(cf. Jn 15:5)* and that we might have life everlasting. He has promised abundant graces to those who come to Him through devotion to the Sacred Heart. There are twelve specific promises which have been taken from the revelations to Saint Margaret Mary:

1. I will give them all the graces necessary for their state in life.
2. I will establish peace in their families.
3. I will console them in their difficulties.
4. I will be their refuge during life and more especially at the hour of death.
5. I will shower abundant blessings on all their undertakings.
6. Sinners will find in my Heart the source of an infinite ocean of mercy.
7. Through devotion to my Heart tepid souls shall become fervent.
8. Fervent souls will rise to great perfection.
9. I will bless every place where a picture of my Heart shall be exposed and honored.
10. I will give to priests the gift of touching the most hardened hearts.
11. Persons who promote this devotion shall have their names written in my Heart forever.
12. I will grant the grace of final repentance to all who receive the Eucharist on the first Friday of nine consecutive months.

It is perhaps this last promise that has had the most noticeable effect. The effects of Jansenism were widespread during the seventeenth century, so that most people thought themselves so unworthy of the Eucharist that they would receive communion only once or perhaps twice a year. It is true that in our fallen nature we are unworthy to receive our Lord in the Eucharist, but in His infinite love, Jesus has offered Himself to us and wants us to avail ourselves of the grace He offers. The promotion of First Friday devotions was singularly successful. The monthly promotion of the Eucharist on the First Friday brought about a new awareness of the need for more frequent communion and an increased devotion to our Lord in the Eucharist.

Throughout the year, we keep the family aware of First Friday devotions and during June we try to give the children a greater awareness of the love of Jesus as manifested by His Sacred Heart. We review the story of the apparitions and explain in some detail the symbolism of the Heart of Jesus as it was shown to Saint Margaret Mary.

The Heart is shown with the wound from the centurion's lance and is surrounded by a crown of thorns. The thorns surrounding the Heart signify that it is the rejection of His love that causes Him the most suffering. The Divine Heart is upon a throne of flame, which represents the unrelenting love the Savior bears for us. The Cross is shown implanted in His Heart where it had been from the first moment of His Incarnation.

We talk about the tender love He bears for us and the rejection that we oftentimes offer Him in return. We talk of reparation, because devotion to the Sacred Heart is a devotion of reparation not only for our own sins but also for the sins of others. Jesus our Lord and Savior asks us through the mystery of this devotion to console His wounded Heart. We do this sometimes by spending time before the Blessed Sacrament and during the month of June we add the words "Sacred Heart of Jesus have mercy on us" to our grace before meals. Thus, our mealtime prayer becomes:

Bless us, O Lord, and these Thy gifts,
which we are about to receive, from Thy bounty,
through Christ our Lord. Amen
Sacred Heart of Jesus, have mercy on us.

We also encourage our children to look occasionally at the picture of the Sacred Heart which hangs in our home and think of the love He bears for us while saying the words, "Jesus I love you." As we ponder the mystery of His love we turn also to the Litany of the Sacred Heart which guides us into the depths and richness of that love.

Another related devotion which has become popular in recent years is the devotion to Divine Mercy as revealed in private revelations to Blessed Faustina Kowalska in the 1930s. Blessed Faustina reported that our Lord appeared with one hand raised in blessing while the other touched His breast and seemed to open His garment. Two rays, one red and the other pale, emanated from the opening. He revealed that the rays represented the Blood and water that flowed from His pierced Heart through the wound in His side.

While both revelations speak of love and mercy, the emphasis is different. The earlier revelations to Saint Margaret Mary concentrated on the unfathomable love Jesus bears for humanity, while the more recent revelations to Blessed Faustina penetrate the depths of mercy which our Lord wishes to bestow on any who will accept His love. He will not force Himself on any soul, but as He revealed to Blessed Faustina, the slightest response from a repentant soul brings forth mercy that defies human understanding.

It is impossible to include a complete description of the Divine Mercy revelations in this work, but there are a few key points worth highlighting:

1. Our Lord asked to have a picture made of Divine Mercy with the red and pale rays shining forth. This picture bearing the inscription "Jesus I trust in You" should be venerated in honor of our merciful Lord.

2. Our Lord asked that we be mindful of His Passion especially at the hour of Divine Mercy (three o'clock in the afternoon). He asked that we pray for sinners at this time even if it is only for a brief moment. He will not refuse the soul that invokes His mercy in this way.

Jesus I Trust in You

3. Our Lord requested that a feast of Divine Mercy be established on the Sunday after Easter. He further requested a novena in preparation for Mercy Sunday to begin on Good Friday and end the Saturday after Easter.

More information about Divine Mercy and the apparitions can be obtained from the Marian Fathers in Stockbridge Massachusetts where they have established the National Shrine of Divine Mercy on top of the beautiful Eden Hill.

Every day at three o'clock the bells ring at the Shrine of Divine Mercy and people gather in the chapel to recite the Divine Mercy chaplet which was also revealed by our Lord. On Mercy Sunday pilgrims gather from all directions as thousands of people come to honor our Lord and His Divine Mercy.

The Divine Mercy devotion is a great blessing in our time. Just as our Lord had saved the devotion to His Sacred Heart to combat the errors of Jansenism in earlier centuries, so it seems He has reserved this devotion to counteract the works of Satan in the last half of the twentieth century as we approach the third millennium.

Although these are private revelations (which we are not bound to believe) the Church has allowed this message of Divine Mercy to be widely disseminated. Private revelation (which must always be measured against the Gospel message and traditional teaching of the magisterium) will often cause the faithful to deepen their acceptance of the Gospel in their lives. Let us pray that this message of Divine Mercy will continue to bring many people into a deeper relationship with our Lord and Savior.

As I experience both His love and His mercy in my life I am often led to pray:

"Sacred Heart of Jesus, I trust in Your Divine Mercy."

XIV

July

Month of the Precious Blood

The redemptive power of the Blood of Christ is a constantly recurring theme throughout the New Testament. In their accounts of the Last Supper, Matthew,
Mark and Luke all record that the New Convenant is in
Christ's Blood, to be poured out for us. John tells us in
Chapter 6 v 53-58 that if we drink His Blood we shall have
eternal life. In Acts 20:28 we find that the Church of God
was acquired at the price of His Blood. Paul, in his letters to
the Ephesians *(1:7; 2:13)*, the Colossians *(1:20)*, the Corinthians *(1 Cor 10:16)* and the Romans *(5:9)* speaks of redemption
in the Blood of Christ. The first letter of Peter and the letter
to the Hebrews also mention the Blood of Christ, as does
John's first letter and the Book of Revelation.

Mention of the Precious Blood of Christ is also found in
the post-Apostolic writings of the early Fathers of the
Church and at least four popes of recent centuries (Pius VII,
Pius XI, Pius XII, John XXIII) have recognized and encouraged devotion to the Precious Blood.

Although one often hears reference to the Blood of Christ

in Scripture, in the liturgy and in song, the real significance is often not fully understood. We have tried through various discussions to develop a greater understanding among our children of Christ's sacrifice on Calvary and the connection between that sacrifice and the Eucharistic Sacrifice which we join in at least weekly. To aid in this discussion we first explain the significance of sacrificial blood, the concept of sacrifice in general and the Passover sacrifice in particular.

To the ancients, blood was almost synonymous with life itself *(cf. Lev 17:11; Deut 12:23)*. When Thomas Jefferson said "the tree of freedom must be watered by the blood of patriots" he was speaking of people dying in defense of their country and when we speak of the blood of martyrs being the seed of the Church we are speaking of people dying for their faith.

Sacrifice always involves a certain surrendering of one's own interests for the good or benefit of another. A parent may make sacrifices so that a child can gain a college education or a person may turn down a promotion that requires relocation in order to remain near an ill or aging parent. A sacrifice for God is also a surrendering of one's own self; not so much for the good or benefit of the Other but as an acknowledgment of our dependence on a Supreme Being. From earliest times, sacrifice and sacrificial offering has been a part of man's relationship with God his Creator *(cf. Gen 4:3; 8:20)*. The ancients recognized their total dependence on God and offered sacrifice as an acknowledgment of that dependence. A sacrificial offering represented in part an offering of themselves and they would sprinkle some of the the sacrificial animal's blood (representing life itself) on the altar as they acknowledged the total dominion of God over all life, including their own.

The ultimate sacrifice is to give one's own life and that is not done easily or altogether willingly. Even Nathan Hale, who said, "I regret that I have but one life to give for my country," would have continued to fight for his life and country if he had had the means at his disposal.

Even Jesus (in the garden of Gethsemane) asked to be relieved of the burden of sacrificing His life, but there was a difference. He truly did offer His life willingly as He said "not my will but yours be done" *(Lk 22:42)*. Certainly He had the means to change the outcome, either by His miraculous powers or by speaking in His own behalf before Pilate *(cf. Mt 27:13-14; Jn 19:9-10)*. This willingness of Jesus to give His life, the ultimate sacrifice, on behalf of others is the real essence and merit of His unique offering. He who had committed no sin and always lived in perfect harmony with the Father willingly and freely offered Himself on behalf of others. He has redeemed us through His submission, through His unselfish giving of self. He has poured out His very life's blood on our behalf. In the words of Isaiah, "Because he surrendered himself to death . . . he shall take away the sins of many and win pardon for their offenses" *(Is 53:12)*.

The Passover sacrifice was the commemoration of the most important event in Jewish history, their deliverance from bondage in Egypt to freedom in the Promised Land. It was also a celebration of God's (Sinai) covenant with His Chosen People. The Sinai covenant is inseparable from the liberation from Egypt and marks the fulfillment of God's promise to Abraham.

Central to the Passover celebration was the sacrificial lamb and sprinkling of the blood of the lamb. It was the sprinkling of the blood of the lamb at the first Passover that saved the lives of first-born Jewish males when the Lord struck down the first-born of all the Egyptians *(cf. Ex 12:1-30)*. Each year as the Passover celebration was repeated, the entire story of the Exodus was recalled and the Israelites praised God for the gift of their deliverance and their covenant with Him.

In the New Covenant, Jesus Christ becomes both priest and victim as He offers Himself as the sacrificial lamb of the New Passover. In the Old Covenant, God offered His Chosen People a deliverance from the bondage of slavery in Egypt to freedom in the Promised Land. In the New Covenant, God offers the New Israel, the new People of God, a deliverance from the bondage of sin to the freedom of new life in the Mystical Body of Christ. At Sinai, Moses sealed the covenant by sprinkling the sacrificial blood on the people saying "This is the blood of the covenant which the LORD has made with you" *(Ex 24:8).* At the Last Supper, Jesus took the cup and said, "this is my blood of the covenant, which will be shed on behalf of many for the forgiveness of sins" *(Mt 26:28)* and then, on the Cross, He poured out His life's blood for us. His death on the Cross was a true sacrifice which has replaced not only the Passover sacrifice but all the ritual sacrifice of the Old Covenant. The letter to the Hebrews develops this concept in some detail and provides much of the theological basis for our understanding of the sacrificial nature of Christ's death on the Cross.

After He proclaimed the cup to be "the new covenant in my blood" *(1 Cor 11:25)* He said, "Do this, as often as you drink it, in remembrance of me" *(1 Cor 11:25),* thereby extending a share in His sacrificial offering to all future generations. The celebration of the Mass is a reenactment of the Last Supper; when the priest says the words of consecration, the wine again becomes the sacrificial Blood of Christ which was poured out for us. Through this mystery of the Eucharist, we actually have a re-creation of the sacrifice on Calvary in which the Body and Blood of Christ are again offered to the Father on our behalf.

In the Precious (sacrificial) Blood of Christ we receive many blessings. Our sins have been forgiven, our salvation has been acquired and we have been offered eternal life.

Another blessing that has come to us through the Precious Blood of Christ is the gift of the Holy Spirit. In the Gospel of John we find the words: "Whoever believes in me, as scripture says:

'Rivers of living water will flow from within him'

He said this in reference to the Spirit that those who came to believe in him were to receive. There was, of course, no Spirit yet, because Jesus had not yet been glorified" *(Jn 7:38-39)*.

From Apostolic times, the Church has understood the *living water* mentioned in the Old Testament and quoted by Jesus as referring to the Holy Spirit, and in particular to the new manifestation of the Holy Spirit on Pentecost. This living water was seen as coming symbolically from the Heart of Jesus in the Blood that flowed from Him as He hung on the Cross. The Holy Spirit did, of course, exist with the Father and the Son from all eternity but we have a more active and universal relationship to humanity in the New Covenant.

During the month of July, we recall the saving qualities of Christ's Precious Blood by a short addition to our normal mealtime blessing:

> *Bless us, O Lord, and these Thy gifts,*
> *which we are about to receive, from Thy bounty,*
> *through Christ our Lord, who has redeemed*
> *us with His Precious Blood. Amen.*

We can also turn to the Litany of the Most Precious Blood of Jesus as we seek a greater insight into the power and protection of the Blood of Christ poured out for our salvation.

XV

August

Month of the Immaculate Heart of Mary

In chapter XII, we discussed devotion to Mary and her place in God's plan in traditional terms as taught by many saints of past centuries. The Second Vatican Council also examined and presented Mary's place in God's plan of salvation as an integral part of the Dogmatic Constitution on the Church. While not intending to give a complete doctrine on Mary, the Council confirmed many of the traditional teachings and specifically allowed the retention of those opinions relating to Our Lady and her special position in God's plan which have not been fully clarified, but have been freely proposed by various theological schools of thought *(cf. D. C. C. #54)*.

The Council placed greater emphasis, however, on Mary as a model of the Church and model for Christian living *(cf. D. C. C. #63 & 65)*. Many writers of recent years have followed this *model* theme as they have attempted to more fully understand Mary's role in God's plan. Mary as *model Christian* is the theme we follow as we ponder the Immaculate

Heart of Mary and look to her to lead us ever closer to her Son Jesus.

The Heart of Mary was the first human heart to know and love our Lord and Savior Jesus Christ. Saint Augustine tells us that she was more blessed in having borne Christ in her heart than in having conceived Him in the flesh. The Heart of Mary is a mother's heart; a mother's heart that loves her Son and a mother's heart that loves her spiritual sons and daughters who make up the Mystical Body of her Son.

The Heart of Mary, like that of her Son, is presented to us as representing the inner being of the person. As noted earlier, the Heart of Jesus represents both the human and the divine and therefore becomes an object of true adoration. In Mary we find only human qualities and our honor and devotion is as a result of the singular graces that God has bestowed upon her.

Devotion to the Heart of Mary, like devotion to the Heart of Jesus, traces its origins back to the Gospel writers. Matthew tells us that the Magi, after a long searching journey found "the child with Mary his mother" (Mt 2:11) and it is with Mary that we too find Jesus. It is this desire to find and know Jesus that brings us to the Heart of Mary. Mary has known Jesus better than any other human being and Luke tells us that Mary kept her memories of Jesus in her Heart (cf. Lk 2:19, 51).

The Heart of Mary, with all its joys and sorrows, becomes our model as we strive to change our own hearts in response to the Good News of Jesus. We might join her first at the Annunciation, as she is confronted by the heavenly messenger. What would our reaction be if confronted by an angel? Would we be frightened by this manifestation of God's power or would we be puffed up with pride over God's "wise choice" in coming to us with His message? Mary receives the news with humility and amazement. Mary, who has unquestioned confidence in God, does not dispute the message but merely asks how it will happen. In light of her commitment to perpetual virginity, she has to know if God is asking for a new and different response. The angel tells her that the Holy Spirit will come upon her and that she will conceive in a way contrary to all natural and biological laws. With trust in her Heart, Mary accepts the word and is no longer troubled; she has complete confidence in God.

Have any of us ever known that kind of faith and trust in God? Would not our response be more like that of Zechariah or Abraham, who were skeptical when presented with an unusual conception in old age? Zechariah asked the Angel Gabriel not how it was to happen but how he was to know it would happen *(cf. Lk 1:18)* while "Abraham prostrated himself and laughed as he said to himself, 'Can a child be born to a man who is a hundred years old? Or can Sarah give birth at ninety?'" *(Gen 17:17)* Zechariah and Abraham, like us, lacked the simple confident faith of Mary. Yes, there is much to learn from the humble and confident Heart of Mary.

But what of Mary's response to the angelic announcement (which in reality was not a command but a request, since God always allows free will and never forces Himself upon anyone)? Mary must have known this call from God, as with every call from God, would include difficulty and hardship. Often in the past those *highly favored* by God were ridiculed, despised and sometimes killed. God's servants rarely find an easy road in this life. Couldn't she take time to think it over? Couldn't she have reservations like Jeremiah *(cf. Jer 1:6; 20:7-10)* Isaiah *(cf. Is 6:5)* or Moses *(cf. Ex 4:1)*? No! Mary's response came from her Immaculate Heart, "I am the handmaid of the Lord. May it be done to me according to your word" *(Lk 1:38)*.

The entire Jewish nation had waited for centuries for the event that was to take place in Mary. All previous generations had prayed and longed for this fulfillment. Mary too must have prayed often for the coming of the Messiah. Mary was to be an integral part of the most important event in the history of her nation and indeed the entire world. During the next nine months the life of the Messiah would be totally dependent on her life's blood. Who could object if she, so highly favored by God, were to expect a little consideration and service from those around her to whom she was about to bring the Savior of the world? But this was not to be Mary's response.

The Angel Gabriel told Mary that her cousin Elizabeth was with child but nowhere is it recorded that he told her to go to visit her; Mary was not commanded or even asked to go. It was the love and compassion of her Heart that prompted her journey into the hill country where Elizabeth lived. Mary's only motivation was to be of service to one who in her old age might be in need of assistance.

As we ponder Mary's unselfish response we might consider our own motivation if placed in a similar situation. Are we not often motivated to have the last word? When someone shares the news of their good fortune, are we not likely to respond with news of our own? Mary has been told that Elizabeth has been favored by God but Mary does not go to announce her greater favor; she goes only to be of service to one who may be in need. Mary does not even announce her favor. It is Elizabeth who announces what she has apparently learned by divine revelation through the action of the Holy Spirit. Elizabeth praises Mary, and Mary, in the humility of her Heart, does not accept it for herself, but rather reflects that praise to the God who has so highly favored her, as she proclaims the words of the beautiful Magnificat (cf. Lk 1:46-55).

In these two stories of the Annunciation and the Visitation Saint Luke shows us the true inner character of Mary's Heart, where we find trust in God as well as loving compassion for other human beings. May God grant us the grace to follow, even in a small way, that wonderful example of the Heart of Mary.

As the months passed and the day of the birth grew closer, a decree was published ordering a census. Joseph and Mary were required to go to Bethlehem to register.

Mary was in no condition to travel and this journey would take several days on the back of a donkey. We might wonder at her reaction when informed of the need for this trip. What would our reaction be if placed in a similar situation? Perhaps we would look for an excuse to avoid such hardship. Surely Joseph would have been saddened to take her on such a journey. Luke makes no mention of any reluctance on Mary's part. Might we not expect that her response to Joseph's announcement echoed the words of Ruth, "wherever you go I will go, wherever you lodge I will lodge" *(Ru 1:16)*? Mary would not have wanted to cause Joseph any additional stress and would have cheerfully accompanied him as she placed her trust in the Lord. Perhaps this story can also bring to mind the words of Paul in his letter to the Romans: "We know that all things work for good for those who love God" *(Rom 8:28)*. In God's plan the census was the occasion for the fulfillment of the Messianic birth in Bethlehem.

We have all experienced or witnessed joy and happiness at the birth of a child, but can we ever imagine the joy that must have been in the Heart of Mary as she brought into the world He who made the world? As we ponder that joy, we might renew our commitment to Jesus in the hope that we too might see Him one day and experience in our hearts the joy of Mary's Heart.

Luke tells us of the shepherds who came in their poverty and Matthew recalls the Magi who came in their splendor. The contrast between the shepherds and the Magi amplified and expanded Mary's understanding of the fullness of her Son's mission, and she rejoiced that all would be called to salvation.

Matthew tells us the Magi brought gifts of gold, frankincense and myrrh. What was Mary's reaction to these gifts? What did she do with them? What would we have done? Perhaps we would have invested for the future; put it away for the child's education, or perhaps used some to make life more bearable. The Gospel makes no mention of what hap-

pened to the gifts and we can never really know, but perhaps Mary gave it away to those who had even less than
she. There is no way to know, but certainly that would be in
keeping with the charity we find always in the Heart of
Mary. It is easy to imagine she would have compassion on
those less fortunate than herself.

In obedience to Jewish law, Mary and Joseph took Jesus
to the Temple to be presented to the Lord. Considering the
joy and celebration that normally accompanies the baptism
of a child in our own culture, we might reasonably assume
that Mary was joyful and happy as she proceeded towards
the Temple in Jerusalem. The unique knowledge that her
Son was the Messiah for which so many generations had
longed and waited would have gladdened her Heart even
more. That joy and exuberance was soon interrupted, as
Mary was confronted by the prophet Simeon.

Upon entering the Temple, Mary and Joseph were met
by Simeon, who took the child in his arms. The prophet
shared his inspired insight regarding the child's future and
then turned to Mary. He told her that a sword (of sorrow)
would pierce her Heart (cf. Lk 2:22-35).

Here for the first time Mary encounters the realization
that those who would share in the joy of the Messiah must
also accept the sacrifice that so often accompanies the joy. To
put it another way, if you would participate in the Resurrection you must first experience the Cross. Mary is a patient
and humble model of acceptance of God's will in whatever
form it takes.

Mary does not have long to wait for the fulfillment of
Simeon's prediction. Joseph is warned in a dream to take
the child and His mother and flee to Egypt. What do you
suppose would be in the heart of a mother who is fleeing to
save her child? Would it be fear and anxiety? Perhaps, but I
propose that Mary's Heart held only trust and confidence in
the ultimate triumph of God's plan. Her knowledge of
God's intervention must have provided great consolation as
they suffered the hardships of the long journey. Mary may

also have felt a bit of compassion for Joseph who responded unselfishly to God's call.

After some number of years, the time came for them to return to their homeland. This must have been a joyous occasion: Reunions with family and friends and the opportunity once again to celebrate the Passover in Jerusalem. But again the joy would be shattered as the prophecy of Simeon (perhaps almost forgotten) came true once more.

When Jesus was about twelve years old, He accompanied Mary and Joseph to Jerusalem for Passover, but without their knowledge He remained behind as they proceeded home. Mary was with the women and young children, while Joseph traveled with the men and older boys, each thinking Jesus was with the other. Imagine the heartache as they met for the evening meal to find Jesus was not with them. They returned to Jerusalem and for three days they searched for Him.

As we meditate on the symbolic rather than the historical aspects of this event, we find meaning for our own lives. The loss or absence of Jesus due to sin or indifference can leave us with a heavy heart; it is only when we bring Jesus back to the center of our lives that we find peace and happiness. When we find Jesus in our hearts, we rejoice even as Mary must have rejoiced at finding Him in the Temple.

Our next Gospel meeting with Mary is at Cana, where John tells us of her compassion and faith (previously discussed in chapter XII). John later tells us of Mary's ordeal at the foot of the Cross where we see the full impact of Simeon's symbolic sword. Mary's Heart is pierced with the sword of sorrow as she maintains her three-hour vigil at the foot of the Cross. She who has always shown love and concern for others is subjected to the humiliation of seeing her Son suffer the punishments of a convicted criminal. The sword pierces even deeper as she considers the innocence of He who is Love Incarnate. Even in this saddest of occasions, the faith and love of Mary's Sorrowful and Immaculate Heart remain steadfast. She does not abandon her Son; she

remains at the foot of the Cross and unites her own sufferings with those of her Son, on our behalf. We too are called
to unite our sufferings and hardships with Christ so that we
might say with Saint Paul, "I rejoice . . . in my flesh I am fill-
ing up what is lacking in the afflictions of Christ on behalf of
his body, which is the church" (Col 1:24) (see also Rom 8:17-
18; 2 Cor 1:4-7; 4:8-10; Phil 3:10).

Mary, who freely cooperated in God's plan at the Annunciation, who brought Jesus into the world at the Nativity,
who guided Him through His early years, who was with
Him at the beginning of His public ministry and stood by
Him at the foot of the Cross, continued as a full participant
in God's plan even after the Resurrection.

Mary, whose prayers for the fulfillment of God's promise
of a Messiah were answered at the Annunciation, turned
her attention and her prayers to the needs of the early
Church. Jesus promised that He would send the Holy Spirit upon the Apostles to strengthen and guide them (cf. Jn
15:26; Acts 1:8). Luke tells us in Acts 1:14 that they devoted
themselves to constant prayer and that Mary was with
them. Mary is again praying for the fulfillment of a divine
promise; Mary is praying for another coming of the Holy
Spirit, the same Holy Spirit who had come upon her and
overshadowed her at the Annunciation. Mary, who brought
Christ into the world and gave Him His human body, now
participates fully in the birth of His Mystical Body, the
Church, at Pentecost.

After Pentecost, we hear no more of Mary's earthly life.
She does not claim any special or exalted position for herself. The ever-humble Mary was content during her earthly
life to pray for her spiritual sons and daughters and remain
in obscurity.

In Heaven, Mary continues to pray and intercede for her
spiritual children. Her only desire is to bring Christ into
their lives and lead them all into full union with her Son. So
desirous is she of leading all people to her Son that she has
even come back to earth on numerous occasions to plead

and beg her children to turn away from sin and indifference and follow her to Jesus. Many of these appearances, such as those at Lourdes, La Salette, Fatima and Knock are well known. There are many others not so well known, but always the message is the same: A call to all of Mary's children to come to her firstborn, Jesus.

I would like to add a few words about just one of these appearances, as I think any discussion of the Immaculate Heart of Mary would be incomplete without mention of the message of Fatima. It was at Fatima that Mary requested devotion to her Immaculate Heart in order to save sinners from Hell.

Mary appeared several times in 1917 to three young shepherd children and told them the war that was going on would end soon but that if people did not turn back to God another even more terrible war would take place. She told these children (who had probably never even heard of Russia) that Russia would spread errors throughout the world and provoke wars and persecution. She said if her requests were heeded, Russia would be converted and there would be peace; if not, the strife would continue and nations would be annihilated. People did not turn back to God and many of the Fatima predictions came true with the advent of World War II and the spread of atheistic Communism throughout much of Europe and Asia.

Despite these dire predictions and the consequences of sin and indifference, there is one part of the Fatima story that has always given me great hope and expectation. Our Lady did not say when or how long we would have to wait, but she did say that in the end her Immaculate Heart would triumph, Russia would be converted and there would be a period of peace in the world. We may well have witnessed the beginning of the fulfillment of that hope when John Paul II was elected pope. He brought with him a great devotion to Mary, sustained by the deep spirituality and faith of the Polish people. Perhaps the rapid (almost miraculous) changes in Eastern Europe that we witnessed

in 1989 and which continue to unfold in this final decade of
the second millennium are the beginning of that period of
peace which the world yearns for. Perhaps now more than
ever we should join in prayer and repentance, so that we
may see the continuation of peaceful revolution and a
return to God.

Mary loves her children as only a mother can. She constantly calls and leads them to Jesus if only we will follow.
During the month of August, we turn to Mary and ask her
through her Immaculate Heart to lead us to Jesus. We try to
give the children some appreciation for Mary as a model of
Christian living and discuss with them the devotion to her
Immaculate Heart. We add a simple invocation to the end of
our grace before meals, so that our mealtime prayer
becomes:

> *Bless us, O Lord, and these Thy gifts,*
> *which we are about to receive,*
> *from Thy bounty, through Christ our Lord. Amen*
> *Immaculate Heart of Mary, show us the way to your Son.*

The Litany of the Blessed Virgin Mary, also known as the
Litany of Loreto (for its place of origin in Loreto Italy) is a
beautiful tribute to the Mother of God which can be used as
an occasional after-meal prayer. Her many titles remind us
of the special graces God has granted to His Holy Mother
and her place in His plan of salvation.

XVI

September

Month of the Holy Spirit

Traditionally, September has been designated the month of the Queen of Martyrs or the month of Our Lady of Sorrows. In our family we have chosen instead to make September the month of the Holy Spirit.

We have several reasons for making this change: While on earth, both before and after His death, Jesus said He would send the Holy Spirit to the Apostles and the Church *(cf. Jn 14:26; 16:7; Lk 24:49; Acts 1:4-5)*. On Pentecost (the birthday of the Church) the Holy Spirit descended upon the Apostles and the others gathered with them, immediately transforming their lives *(cf. Acts 2)*. The Holy Spirit was well known in the early Church and was the driving force behind the rapid expansion of Christianity *(cf. Acts 2:4, 41; 10:44; 20:28; 1 Cor 2:4; 2 Tim 1:7, 14; Jude 1:20)*. In recent centuries, devotion to the Holy Spirit has not been as strong as some of the other popular devotions. That, however, seems to be changing in our time.

Past decades have witnessed a tremendous rekindling of interest in the Holy Spirit, both within and outside the

Catholic Church. This interest has manifested itself in the Charismatic Renewal of recent years. Devotion to the Holy Spirit is certainly one of the most fruitful and timely of all devotions and for this reason, we wanted to reserve a full month for our family to focus on the Holy Spirit.

But why September? The most obvious month would be the month in which Pentecost falls. There are some practical problems in choosing a month to coincide with Pentecost, since this feast does not occur in the same month every year. Some years it comes in May and other years it occurs in June. These months already contain two of the better known devotions, the month of Mary and the month of the Sacred Heart.

As we looked for a special month for the Holy Spirit, September seemed particularly appropriate. The traditional monthly designations for September are less well known than most other months. September also falls between two months which are designated for more well known Marian devotions. But the overriding reason for September is that it is the month in which the children go back to school; an ideal time to ask the Holy Spirit for three of His better known gifts, namely wisdom, knowledge and understanding.

During this time, we ask God the Holy Spirit, the third person of the Blessed Trinity, to enlighten us and lead us on life's road and in particular to aid the children during the school year so they may understand the right relationship between their secular studies, their day-to-day life and growth in their spiritual life. Throughout the month of September we precede our grace before meals with the following prayer:

Come Holy Spirit, enlighten our minds;
fill the hearts of Thy faithful
and kindle in them the fire of Thy love.

Also during September, we try to find time for two or three after-meal discussions. We briefly review the Pentecost story, then examine the gifts of the Holy Spirit and the action of the Holy Spirit in our lives. We look at both the ordinary or traditional gifts which we find listed in Isaiah (*cf. Is 11:2*), as well as the extraordinary or charismatic gifts described in Paul's letters to the Corinthians and Romans (*cf. Rom 12:3-8; 1 Cor 12-14*).

Some years ago, while attending a parish mission, we heard a memorable talk about the indwelling of the Holy Spirit. As the mission priest began his talk, he shared an observation which he had gained through years of pastoral service: The difference between a mediocre Christian life and a fervent Christian life, he said, is occasioned by the recognition and realization of the indwelling of the Holy Spirit. We have all received the Holy Spirit by virtue of our baptism and confirmation, but as we become aware of the significance of that gift, our lives begin to change. We realize the tremendous love God bears for each of us and we recognize the inherent obligation to live a truly Christian life. As we try to live that obligation, we are drawn closer to God, our fervor increases and we become more fully aware of the action of the Holy Spirit in our lives.

It is our hope that by focusing attention on the Holy Spirit at this time, we will ignite a spark of recognition that will be fanned into a flame of realization as our children grow into adulthood.

Ordinary Gifts of the Holy Spirit . . .

WISDOM is the gift which enables a person to make decisions that are consistent with the will of God. Wisdom allows a person to live life with a proper perspective and to realize that all the answers do not lie within one's own being. Through the gift of wisdom, we find a proper relationship to God and our fellow man as well as realize our own place in the world.

For a greater appreciation of the value of wisdom it is helpful to read the first chapter of the second Book of Chronicles. In verse 7, we read that God told Solomon to make a request and He would grant it. Solomon could have

asked for riches, power or glory but he asked instead for wisdom which God granted him in abundance (*cf. 2 Chr 1:10-12*). Chapters 6, 7 and 8 of the Book of Wisdom are also helpful and enlightening.

Wisdom is truly a gift from God. In the words of Solomon, "this, too, was prudence, to know whose is the gift" (*Wis 8:21*).

UNDERSTANDING is that gift by which God grants deeper (and sometimes personal) meaning to revealed truths. Many people have experienced the gift of understanding in the reading of Sacred Scripture. People who for years avoided reading the "dull", "dry" or "uninteresting" Bible suddenly find new meaning in the Word of God.

Sometimes when we feel a particular spiritual or psychological need, we are drawn to the Scriptures and often God seems to provide just the right word at the right time. I experienced a dramatic and personal example of this gift. One of my children had misbehaved and my response was somewhat out of proportion to the incident. One word led to another and it turned into a rather bad scene. The next day while at work I reflected on the incident and felt somewhat distressed about it. I spontaneously reached for the Bible which I always keep close at hand and randomly opened to one of almost 1,400 pages. The page I opened to contained the fifteenth chapter of Proverbs and the words my eyes fell upon were:

"A mild answer calms wrath,
but a harsh word stirs up anger." *(Prov 15:1)*

There wasn't anything new in that statement; the truth of those words was painfully evident from the previous day. And yet, through the gift of understanding, I immediately knew that those words contained a gentle call from a loving God, and that evening I was able to repair the hurt I'd caused.

The gift of **KNOWLEDGE** allows us to see created things in their proper perspective and enables us to avoid an unhealthy materialistic attitude. We know there are certainly legitimate material needs, but we also know that it is of little profit if we gain the whole world and suffer the loss of our soul.

Through the gift of **COUNSEL**, the Holy Spirit assists us in choosing a proper course of action based on our enlightenment through the gifts of wisdom, understanding and knowledge.

Through **FORTITUDE** we are enabled to continue on our properly chosen course of action, even in the face of severe adversity.

PIETY allows us to see the work of God in all creation and develops an attitude of love toward our neighbor.

FEAR OF THE LORD instills within us a deep respect for God and leads us to avoid offending He who has loved us so much.

There are many well known people who have exhibited one or more of these gifts in their lives and we have found it helpful to discuss some of them with the children.

The spirit of wisdom can be found in abundance in the person of Pope John XXIII, who knew his own unique place in the world. He was expected in his old age to be a "caretaker" pope as the Church made the transition from the long reign of Pius XII to a successor capable of bringing the Church to a new position in the modern world. Pope John was guided by the wisdom of the Holy Spirit and knew the Church could not wait, but he also knew he could not effect the renewal by himself. He initiated the Second Vatican Council and thus began the process of bringing the Church fully into the twentieth century.

The gift of piety is perhaps best exemplified by the love of Mother Teresa of Calcutta for the poorest of the poor. Mother Teresa (perhaps more clearly than any other living individual) sees in each person a unique creation of God. In her profound reverence for each individual, she serves God and constantly witnesses to the love of Christ. Not all of us are called to serve in the unique way of Mother Teresa, but we are all called to see the handiwork of God in our neighbor.

Martin Luther King Jr. provides another example of the gifts of the Holy Spirit. Certainly he must have been enlightened by the gifts of wisdom, understanding and knowledge as he was guided by the gift of counsel to choose non-violent resistance to racial segregation. But, perhaps his most notable gift was fortitude, sustained by the realization of the indwelling of the Holy Spirit. He battled against great odds, constantly facing discouragement and adversity. He and his family were continually threatened and he was jailed several times. During this long ordeal there were many temptations to give up. Through it all, he was sustained by the awareness that he was not alone; God was with him through the inner presence of the Holy Spirit as he continued on his chosen course of non-violent protest.

Extraordinary Gifts of the Holy Spirit . . .

The gifts of wisdom, understanding, knowledge, counsel, fortitude, piety and fear of the Lord are given to all of us according to our needs as an aid for our pilgrimage through life. There are other gifts of the Holy Spirit which are extraordinary and referred to as "charismatic" gifts. They are given not for the individual but rather for the benefit of others and for building up the Church. These gifts are not given to all, but are found among certain individuals according to the (spiritual) needs of the community.

Paul's first letter to the Corinthians (Chapters 12, 13, 14) and his letter to the Romans (Chapter 12) provide some insight into some of these gifts. While not attempting a complete study of the charismatic gifts, we mention some of them in our September discussions in order to make the children aware of their existence and purpose.

The gift of **HEALING** is perhaps one of the most remarkable phenomenon of our times. Catholics have always believed in the power of God to heal physical, mental or spiritual illnesses, but have not often expected it. While we accepted the miracles of Lourdes, we often looked askance at so called "faith healers." The past two decades have seen a profound change in the attitude of many people. The tremendously powerful action of God working through a human being has shown us once again that the Lord works when He wills and where He wills and that His actions cannot be contained in a box bound by older attitudes.

We try to impress upon our children that while the cure of terminal cancer or crippling rheumatoid arthritis is a wonderful and dramatic manifestation of God's love, the real power of the gift of healing is also manifested in those instances of

inner healing, where God removes psychological hurts, preju-
dices and fears. It is often easy to overlook the real value of
God's gifts if we don't see sensational results. Sometimes we
are looking for a physical healing and God chooses instead to
perform a miracle of inner healing. We should always remember that these gifts come from a good and loving God who
knows our needs better than we know ourselves.

While the recognized gift of healing and an authentic
healing ministry may only be given to a few, we are all
called to be instruments of God's healing power. Whenever
we take the time to be genuinely interested in another person's problems or fears, the love of Jesus shines through us
and it is that love which can heal many hearts.

PROPHECY is another charismatic gift which is often misunderstood. Many people think of prophecy as predicting the future, when in fact the real essence of prophecy is the proclamation of religious truth. There may be some prediction, but it is generally secondary to the main message. This was true of the biblical prophets of the Old Testament and is still true of those who exercise the gift of prophecy today. In Old Testament times the purpose and mission of the prophet was to call the people of Israel back to faithful observance of the law of God. The attitudes and actions of the people had changed over several generations and the prophets became a visible national conscience who would not allow the people to ignore their obligations to their God.

When people speak of prophecy today they are usually referring to the exercise of the gift within the setting of a prayer meeting. The message is often one of encouragement such as "I love you my children" or "Turn back to me and I will give you life." The speaker or "prophet" will generally speak in the first person and deliver words received through the inspiration of the Holy Spirit. Strictly speaking, there is no way to prove that any prophetic utterance is true prophecy, but often people experience a spiritual uplift as the words are received. Often, it seems that just the right word is spoken at just the right time.

A prophetic message may also be delivered to an entire nation rather than just a single prayer group. Martin Luther King Jr.'s "I have a dream" speech is seen by many to be a real prophetic message. In this speech, you find a certain element of prediction and hope for the future, but the real essence of the message was a call to the observance of the Divine Law of love of neighbor.

The action of the Holy Spirit is limitless and there are many other gifts which can be discussed and examined, however, it is beyond the scope of this work to treat them all in detail. Your local Christian bookstore should have several good books which can provide additional instruction for those who desire it.

Faith, Hope and Charity . . .

No discussion of the gifts of the Holy Spirit would be complete without at least mentioning faith, hope and charity (or "love" as it is generally translated today). In Chapter 13 of his first letter to the Corinthians, Paul tells us that all else will pass, but these three will last and that the greatest gift is love.

The basic, underlying principle in the teachings of Jesus is love: love of God and love of neighbor. At the end of His public ministry Jesus gave His disciples a new commandment when He said "love one another as I love you" *(Jn 15:12)*. Jesus not only gave us the commandment to love but He also gave a completely new dimension to the word love.

To understand the Christian view of love it is helpful to look at the Greek language, in which most of the New Testament was originally written. The Greeks had three separate words which could be translated as the word "love" in English. The word "eros" referred to sensual and sexual desire and self gratification, while a higher form of love was expressed by the word "philos." Philos referred primarily to brotherly love or the love of parents for their children. But even philos does not capture the true meaning of Christian love, and so we find in the New Testament the word "agape" which is defined as spontaneous self-giving love expressed freely without calculation of cost or gain to the giver or merit on the part of the receiver. That is our calling as Christians, to love one another with an agape love. That is the love so eloquently described by Paul in 1 Cor 13:4-7.

To love in that way does not come easily to our fallen human nature. We must rely on the Holy Spirit to aid us in unselfishly loving our neighbor. As we learn to love one another, through the action of the Holy Spirit, we will find happiness, joy and that peace which the world cannot give. In the words of Saint John of the Cross, "Where there is no love, put love and you will find love."

XVII

October

Month of the Rosary

Strings of beads have been used for counting prayers in many cultures and religions for thousands of years. Marco Polo was surprised to find the King of Malabar using a string of 104 precious stones to count prayers in the thirteenth century. Saint Francis Xavier and his companions were equally astonished to find a similar practice among the Buddhists of Japan. The use of prayer beads is particularly widespread among the Moslems, who use strings of 33, 66 or 99 beads. The use of prayer-counting devices among Christians can be traced back at least to the fourth century although the Rosary as we know it today seems to have developed some centuries later.

There is a popular legend that traces the origin of our present Rosary to Saint Dominic (1170-1221). The legend relates a vision in which Our Lady gave the Rosary to Saint Dominic with instructions to preach it among the people as an antidote to heresy and sin. While correct in its instruction that Our Lady has asked for devotion to the Rosary and that it is an antidote to heresy and sin, there does not seem to be

any historical evidence to support this legend. The beginnings of the development of the Rosary predate Saint
Dominic by some years, and there is no evidence of Domini-
can involvement until the time of Blessed Alan de la Roche
in the latter part of the fifteenth century. Additionally, early
accounts of the life of Saint Dominic all omit any reference
to the Rosary.

Rather than being the result of a single revelation, the
Rosary seems to have had a gradual development over a long
period of time and in a number of widespread locations.
Reciting or singing the psalms was widely practiced as an
early Christian (monastic) form of daily prayer. Widespread
illiteracy among the lay brothers prevented them from joining
the choir monks as they chanted all 150 (or 50) psalms. The
lay brothers were allowed to substitute a series of 50 or 150
Pater Nosters (Our Fathers) in place of the 50 or 150 psalms.
This practice became quite popular and we find in the *Ancient
Customs of Cluny*, collected in 1096 that at the death of any
brother, every priest was to offer Mass and every non-priest
was either to say 50 psalms or to repeat 50 times the Pater
Noster. The popularity of this form of prayer is attested to by
the widespread existence of craft guilds whose members were
known as "paternosterers" after their occupation of making
prayer beads for counting the 50 repetitions of the Our Father.

Early in the twelfth century interest developed in the
Angelic Salutation *(Lk 1:28)* which the Angel Gabriel
delivered as God's own word of greeting to Mary at the
Annunciation. What more perfect way could there be for
Mary's spiritual children to greet her than to repeat God's
own greeting as recorded in the Gospel of Luke? This
greeting, generally referred to as the *Hail Mary*, lent itself
quite naturally to repetition. People soon began to use the
Pater Noster beads to count repetitions of the Angelic
Salutation. By the latter half of the twelfth century, it had
become common practice to add Elizabeth's greeting *(Lk
1:42)* so that the repetitive greeting became: Hail Mary full
of grace the Lord is with thee; blessed art thou among

women and blessed is the fruit of thy womb. Amen. The Name of Jesus and the invocation were added at a later date. From the twelfth century the practice of repeating the Hail Mary became widespread. One example of the popularity of the practice was Saint Louis (1214-1270) king of France who is said to have repeated this greeting fifty times each day.

The real essence of the Rosary devotion as we know it today is the meditation on certain events in the life of our Lord. The addition of Rosary meditations came much later in the Rosary's development. The first instance of this addition seems to be in the writings of a Carthusian known as Dominic the Prussian (1382-1461), who added a meditation to each of the 150 Hail Marys.

While Our Lady's Rosary did not originate with Saint Dominic, his spiritual sons, the Dominicans, did exert a great influence in spreading this devotion. In the latter half of the fifteenth century, Blessed Alan de la Roche began to preach devotion to the Rosary and established many Rosary confraternities. Alan met with great success; it was because of his influence that the Dominicans became promoters of the Rosary.

Our Lady has approved and requested recitation of the Rosary at Lourdes and Fatima, where she specifically asked that people meditate on the fifteen Mysteries of the Rosary.

There are many books and pamphlets which can help one understand the Mysteries and aid in meditation. One of the most helpful is the *Scriptural Rosary* published by the Christianica Center in Glenview, Illinois. This little book offers a Scripture verse which can be read with each Hail Mary. Ten verses taken together then tell the story of one of the fifteen Mysteries.

We have encouraged our children to use the Scriptural Rosary and have found that it has increased their awareness and understanding. We have also used the Scriptural Rosary with our mealtime prayers during May and October. Each evening as we gather for dinner, we begin with an Our

Father, then we read the ten Scripture verses for one of the Mysteries and follow them with a single Hail Mary and a Glory Be. Some may argue we are cheating and haven't really said the Rosary but we have found this to be an effective and painless way to introduce the Rosary to the children and have observed over the years that they find times of their own choosing to say the complete Rosary. During the first half of the month we take the fifteen Mysteries in order, and then allow the children to pick one of their favorites on each of the remaining days of the month.

The Scriptural Rosary has helped make the Rosary more meaningful to us. We've found it to be particularly beneficial for anyone who has difficulty meditating on the Mysteries. The following reflections and prayers may also aid in meditation:

The First Joyful Mystery

The Annunciation

REFLECTION: At the Annunciation, Mary became the spiritual mother of all mankind. In the beginning, God created Adam and Eve and gave them His plan for happiness. Tempted by Satan, Adam and Eve rejected that plan through a sin of pride. Through that rejection, sin and death entered the world. Even though man rejected God's plan for happiness, God did not abandon him. God devised a new plan and what the first Eve lost through pride the New Eve, Mary, gained back through humility. God asked Mary to be the mother of the Savior; He presented a new plan for salvation to Mary and Mary freely accepted God's plan with the words, "May it be done to me according to your word" (*Lk 1:38*). That plan must have sounded strange to her, but in the full knowledge of who she was and who He was, Mary humbly accepted His plan without reservations. She freely accepted a dual role as "Godmother," that is the "Mother of God" and "spiritual mother" to all mankind.

PRAYER: Mary, my Godmother, mother of my Savior, my own spiritual mother, come into my life and announce to me the Good News of your Son Jesus just as the Angel Gabriel announced the Good News to you so many years ago. Strengthen me, Mary, through your prayers and obtain for me the grace to accept that Good News without reservation, just as you accepted it at the first Annunciation.

The Second Joyful Mystery

The Visitation

REFLECTION: In Mary's visit to Elizabeth, we find a wonderful example of unselfish charity and service, and something more: Luke, through the inspiration of the Holy Spirit, has recorded for us a *type* of Mary's role in God's plan for salvation. Mary brings Jesus (still in her womb) to Elizabeth and Elizabeth is "filled with the holy Spirit" *(Lk 1:41).*

Mary, in God's plan, brought Jesus into the world, that the world might know salvation and new life. Mary continues through her prayers and intercession to cooperate in God's plan of bringing Jesus into the world. If we turn to her, she will bring Him more fully into our lives.

PRAYER: Mary, we beseech you to come and visit us. Bring your Son into our lives, that we might come to know Him better and be filled with His Holy Spirit. Then we too might proclaim with Elizabeth, "blessed is the fruit of your womb. And how does this happen to me, that the mother of my Lord should come to me?" *(Lk 1:42-43).*

The Third Joyful Mystery

The Nativity

REFLECTION: The birth, into the world, of He who made the world is the best-known and best-loved of all the

Gospel stories. That story which never grows old is retold around the world each year, continuing to bring hope to mankind.

Jesus, the Prince of Peace, was born into the world almost 2,000 years ago. Still there is not peace in the world and we wonder: Why? Perhaps it is because people will not allow Jesus to be born into their hearts. He holds all the answers, He is "the way and the truth and the life" (*Jn 14:6*), but He will not force Himself into any heart. He did not force Himself into the world; He asked for the cooperation of Mary and waited for her free response. He will not force Himself on us, but waits for us to open our hearts in response to His constant call. For her response, Mary was blessed with the first Christmas and the birth of the Savior into the world. For our response, we will be blessed with a re-creation of Mary's blessing, as the Savior is reborn into the world of our hearts.

Let us resolve that at the next commemoration of the Nativity, we will wish our friends and loved ones not a "Merry Christmas" but a "Mary's Christmas", in the hope that they, too, will experience the birth of Jesus into the world of their hearts.

PRAYER: Come Lord Jesus and be born into our hearts and remain with us always, that we might experience that peace which the world cannot give.

The Fourth Joyful Mystery

The Presentation

REFLECTION: Jesus was entrusted to Mary's care; He was her child and she loved Him as any mother loves her child. And yet she knew that one day she must give Him up for the salvation of the world. In obedience to the Jewish law and in accordance with God's plan, Mary took her Son to the Temple to present Him to the Lord.

PRAYER: Mary, Queen of All Hearts, come and present your Son Jesus in the temple of our hearts, that He might grow in us and we in Him, so that one day we might say with Saint Paul "I live, no longer I, but Christ lives in me" *(Gal 2:20).*

The Fifth Joyful Mystery

The Finding of Jesus in the Temple

REFLECTION: Saint Augustine said "No man loses Thee unless he goes from Thee." This was true of Mary as well; her loss of Jesus was occasioned by her going out of Jerusalem while Jesus remained behind. We too lose Jesus when we go away from Him through sin and indifference. Mary searched for three days and finally found Jesus in the Temple. Although our search often takes longer, in reality it should be much easier. We have only to open our eyes and see our brothers and sisters in need to find Jesus, for He said "whatever you did for one of these least brothers of mine, you did for me" *(Mt 25:40).*

PRAYER: Lord, Jesus, come and be found in the temple of our hearts and remain with us always. Help us to grow in love for one another, that we might see you more clearly in our brothers and sisters.

The First Sorrowful Mystery

The Agony in the Garden

REFLECTION: The night before He died, Jesus went to the Mount of Olives to pray. He knew the fate that awaited Him and He felt the weight of the sins of the world. Not His sins, but ours, yours and mine. He asked His disciples to pray with Him for an hour, but they fell asleep, so He suffered His anguish alone. Those who were closest to Him would not share the burden, but through the mystery of

time and eternity we have the opportunity to share mystically in His ordeal. When we spend an hour with Him in prayer, we lighten His burden and when we turn away from Him we make it more difficult.

PRAYER: Lord, give us the strength to watch one hour with you. Show us the weight of our own sins, that we might resolve more firmly to avoid those occasions in the future. Give us the grace, Lord, to persevere in our commitment to follow You into the Father's Kingdom.

The Second Sorrowful Mystery

The Scourging at the Pillar

REFLECTION: The dictionary defines "stripe" as a blow struck with a whip or rod, as in a flogging. Some 700 years before the scourging, the prophet Isaiah foretold: "the LORD laid upon him the guilt of us all" *(Is 53:6)* and "by his stripes we were healed" *(Is 53:5)*. Jesus willingly accepted the scourging and gave Himself as an offering for our sins.

In former times, a "whipping boy" was one who was

brought up as a companion to a prince and punished in his place for any misdeeds. The rationale was that the misdeed could not go unpunished, but no one would dare lay a hand on the royal prince who would one day be king. If you think of that situation, could you ever imagine the prince offering to change positions with the whipping boy and accept punishment for the boy's misdeeds? Oh, there might be some noble youth who would accept the punishment for his own offenses, but certainly not for those of another. And yet, that is exactly what Jesus has done for us. It is the King of Kings, our Lord and Master, our Maker who has offered Himself as our "whipping boy" in order to heal us from the guilt of our sins.

Let us follow the example of Jesus and offer our own daily trials and tribulations to the Father in reparation for our own sins and those of our brothers and sisters. Let us resolve to praise the Lord whenever we are subjected to any kind of unjust humiliation or hardship by a fellow human being. Let us resolve to pray for, rather than complain about, those who do us harm. This does not mean that we become masochistic or that we fail to defend ourselves at times, but we should try to recognize those times when prayer and silence are the better course of action.

PRAYER: Lord, Jesus, by Your stripes we have been healed. We thank You for Your gift of new life and salvation. Teach us to love one another as You have loved us and help us to reach out in service to those around us.

The Third Sorrowful Mystery

The Crowning with Thorns

REFLECTION: Jesus was, is and ever will be the King of Kings and yet He never sought any earthly kingdom or any earthly crown. His only desire was to give each and every one of us a lasting crown of glory as He called us into the Kingdom of His Father. What a cruel hoax that One so innocent, One who was truly the King of Kings, One who out of love came into the world as the servant of servants *(cf. Jn 13:1-15)* should be subjected to such humiliation and ridicule. And yet, as our Lord told Saint Margaret Mary, it is not the crown of thorns placed on His head by the soldiers that gives Him pain; rather it is the crown of thorns fashioned by sin, rejection and indifference that we continually place upon His Sacred Heart. He offers us a crown of glory and we give Him a crown of thorns. He offers us love and we offer Him rejection and indifference. He offers us life and we choose death.

PRAYER: Jesus, You are our King, come and reign over our hearts; give us the grace to persevere in love and service that we might one day receive our everlasting crown of glory. Show us the way to the Father's Kingdom and let us join the angelic choirs in their song of everlasting praise.

The Fourth Sorrowful Mystery

The Carrying of the Cross

REFLECTION: Jesus told us that we must take up our cross daily and follow Him *(cf. Lk 9:23)* but He has not asked us to do anything He has not already done. For Jesus, the Cross was the physical cross of crucifixion; for us it is the symbolic cross of life's struggles. In carrying the Cross Jesus left us a marvelous example for our own life. Jesus willingly accepted His Cross on our behalf. We must learn to do the same.

There is another lesson to be learned as well. If we look at the traditional fourteen Stations of the Cross we find, curiously enough, that three of them are the same: (III) Jesus falls the first time; (VII) Jesus falls a second time; (IX) Jesus falls a third time. Perhaps it is the inspiration of the Holy Spirit that prompted the Church to include this repetition; we should ponder its wisdom and meaning. The Cross that Jesus carried represented the sins of the world. The Church has portrayed Him falling under the weight of (our) sin several times, but each time He got up and continued the struggle. We too fall under the influence of sin, but just as Jesus got up each time, so too must we rise up and continue the struggle. Jesus has overcome sin on our behalf and in Him we too shall overcome.

PRAYER: Jesus, You said, "my yoke is easy, and my burden light" *(Mt 11:30);* help us, Jesus, to carry our daily cross. Lighten our burden, that we may finally persevere and overcome as You have overcome.

The Fifth Sorrowful Mystery

The Crucifixion

REFLECTION: On the Cross Jesus becomes both priest and victim: "he gives his life as an offering for sin" *(Is 53:10).* "And he shall take away the sins of many, and win pardon for their offenses" *(Is 53:12).* Jesus died for our sins. We "have been purchased at a price" *(1 Cor 6:20).* That price is the Blood of Christ which is precious beyond all price *(cf. 1 Pet. 1:18-19).* We who were slaves to sin now belong to Him; He has paid the price and purchased us, but He does not claim us as slaves. Rather, He offers us our freedom and invites us to become beloved sons and daughters of His Father, if only we will follow Him. If we refuse and reject His offer of freedom, we return to our former condition of slaves of sin. The choice is ours: We can accept the invitation and become sons and daughters in freedom and heirs to the Kingdom or we can refuse and live the life of runaway slaves.

PRAYER: We belong to You Jesus. You have bought and paid for us with Your Precious Blood on Calvary. Come into our lives, Lord Jesus, and claim us as Your own, that we might live in You and You in us.

The First Glorious Mystery

The Resurrection

REFLECTION: In the last five discussions, we have looked at the Passion and suffering of Jesus. Perhaps so much talk of sin, guilt and sacrifice is depressing to some, but there is always hope; after the Cross comes the Resurrection.

After almost two thousand years of Christian traditon and belief, it is easy to say "He is risen" without so much as a second thought. Perhaps for some it is just a pious statement with little more meaning than "magi from the east arrived in Jerusalem" *(Mt 2:1)* or "there were shepherds in that region" *(Lk 2:8)*. For most of today's Christians, the real meaning and full impact is hidden by twenty centuries of familiarity. To gain a real appreciation of the words "He is risen" requires one to mentally re-create and relive the experience as the Apostles must have experienced it.

The Apostles left everything to follow Jesus and had been with Him almost three years. Their expectations had been raised to great heights, which only served to accentuate the seeming defeat of the Crucifixion. At the very pinnacle of His ministry, everything seemed to fall apart. He was acclaimed by the people, followed by great crowds and yet He died almost alone.

The Messianic hopes of the Apostles centered on the restoration of Israel to earthly power and they expected to have a part in the ruling of the new Israel. As they watched Jesus among the crowds and witnessed His power, they must have been moved by visions of grandeur. The fulfillment of the age-old hope of every Jew since the time of King David was so close they could feel it in their bones. This excitement was in the very air that they breathed. How they must have longed to get on with the restoration of the kingdom as they anticipated the positions of prominence they were expecting. And just as the Son of Man was about to come into His glory, everything came to a crashing halt. Nothing was happening the way they expected.

First there was the vague talk about suffering (cf. Mk 8:31; 10:32-34; Mt 16:21; 17:22; 20:17-19; Lk 9:22, 44-45; 18:31-34). In their anticipation of an earthly Kingdom, they had somehow missed Isaiah 53 and Psalm 22. Then He told them it would be better if He went away (cf. Jn 16:7) and at the Last Supper He said "I have eagerly desired to eat this Passover with you before I suffer" (Lk 22:15).

What was this recurring theme of suffering? Wasn't the restoration of the kingdom about to take place? They had just experienced His triumphal entry into Jerusalem. Wasn't it time to forget about suffering and get on with the business of restoration? They must have been confused and full of wonder. Then came the Agony in the Garden, for which they couldn't even stay awake. What must have gone through their minds as the soldiers came to arrest Jesus? Peter was ready to fight—he had come too far to let it all go now. But Jesus wouldn't hear of it. He knew (even if Peter refused to listen and understand) where the Kingdom really was. Then there was the desertion by the Apostles, the mock trial and the walk to Calvary. Everything was going wrong—this was not the way it was supposed to be. Jesus was lifted up on the Cross and all their hopes hung there, seemingly helpless. Many jeered: "He saved others; he cannot save Himself" (Mk 15:31). With the exception of John and His mother, they could not bear even to watch, and so they scattered. And then Jesus died and was placed in a tomb. It was all over. He had raised Lazarus but no one could raise Him.

What were they to do now? They were crushed beyond belief. Their hopes had been dashed to the ground. They were confused and fearful for their own lives. The best they could expect would be ridicule—they would be laughing-stocks for having put their trust in a man. The worst? They might be rounded up for a similar fate.

Close your eyes for a moment and just imagine, if you can, the feelings of the Apostles at that time.

What anguish they must have experienced during those three days. They had not only lost their friend and teacher but their whole lives and all their expectations had been buried in the tomb. Think of it—it must have seemed like the end of the world for them.

Then the women came with the words "He is alive." The Apostles would not believe this "nonsense"; it must have seemed like a cruel hoax. He had said He would come back—but that was nonsense—they were rational men—they knew better than to believe some hysterical women. And yet, Peter could not contain himself. Perhaps it was the irrationality of grief, perhaps he was grasping at straws, but he had to see the tomb. He peered in and saw only the wrappings. What went through Peter's mind at that point? Luke tells us "he went home amazed at what had happened" (*Lk 24:12*). Could He be alive? No, that was too

much to hope for. And then He came and stood in their midst and said "Peace be with you." *(Lk 24:36)*. Can you imagine that moment? The euphoria that must have welled up among the Apostles! It must have been anything but peaceful, and yet, what peace it must have brought as they exclaimed He *is* alive!

HE IS RISEN

ALLELUIA!

Jesus overcame sin and death. With Him and in Him, we too can overcome sin and death. The Resurrection of Jesus Christ is our hope for eternal life.

PRAYER: Jesus, our Resurrected Lord and Savior, come into our lives and lead us into the Kingdom. Help us to follow You, willingly bearing all the crosses in our lives, so that we too might finally experience the true joy of the Resurrection.

The Second Glorious Mystery

The Ascension

REFLECTION: Jesus has ascended into Heaven. This is the completion and the fulfillment of the glory of the Resurrection. He has returned to the Father from whence He came. From Heaven He is able to transcend all restrictions of time, space and matter. He is able to be with each one of us simultaneously and to act with us and in us to the extent that we open ourselves to Him. He will not force Himself on us but waits for our response. He tells us in the Book of Revelation, "Behold, I stand at the door and knock. If anyone hears my voice and opens the door, [then] I will enter his house" *(Rev 3:20)*. He continually knocks at the door of our hearts, waiting to be let in. He wants to work in our lives, but He waits for an invitation.

He has ascended into Heaven but He still lives and acts in the world. His earthly body has been glorified and gone to Heaven, but He has a new body in the world. He wants that body to be more fully present in this world and He asks us to make Him present when He says "you will be my witnesses in Jerusalem, throughout Judea and Samaria, and to the ends of the earth" *(Acts 1:8)* and "Whoever listens to you listens to me" *(Lk 10:16).*

He has many ways of being present in the world. He will come and dwell in our hearts if we open them to Him, but He desires to be present even to those who will not open their hearts. That is why He asks us to make Him known, to show His love in the world and to be witnesses to Him throughout the world.

PRAYER: Jesus, come into our lives, come and dwell in our hearts and help us to grow in Your love, that we might be witnesses to that love. Build us up in Your body, Jesus, that we might show Your saving presence to those whose hearts are closed through sin and indifference. Grant us the grace, O Lord, to open the hearts of others to Your saving grace, that one day we might all be joined together in a Heavenly hymn of praise.

The Third Glorious Mystery

The Descent of the Holy Spirit

REFLECTION: The Apostles are again filled with expectation. The crushing defeat of the Crucifixion has been turned into victory by the Resurrection. Jesus has overcome death, and the Apostles have new hope; but still they do not understand. Jesus had told them of the need to suffer *(cf. Mk 8:31),* that they must be the servant of all *(cf. Jn 13:12-15; Mk 9:35)* and that the first would be last *(cf. Lk 14:8-11).* He told them that they did not belong to the world *(cf. Jn 15:19)* and His Kingdom was not of this world *(cf. Jn 18:36),* but still they asked, "Lord, are you at this time going to restore the kingdom to Israel?" *(Acts 1:6).* They were still looking for an earthly kingdom, so persistent was their misunderstanding. Jesus told them He would send another who would

teach them everything and remind them of all that He had told them *(cf. Jn 14:26)* and now He told them again to wait for the Holy Spirit *(cf. Acts 1:4-5)*.

When the day of Pentecost came, they were all together, praying and waiting for the fulfillment of another promise they still did not understand. Israel had waited centuries and prayed for the fulfillment of the first promise and now they had to wait again. "How long, O Lord?" This time it would not be so long.

The same virgin whose faithful prayer hastened the fulfillment of the original promise was with them, joining her prayers for the fulfillment of this promise as well. Mary and the Apostles prayed, and then a wonderful thing happened. The same Holy Spirit who had overshadowed Mary at the Annunciation now came upon all of them. Now they were enlightened, finally they understood all that Jesus had told them. They were so filled with joy and wonder that they began to praise God and proclaim the advent of the Kingdom, the New Israel. So overwhelmed were they that some of the crowd thought they were drunk on new wine, until Peter got up and explained what had happened. These men who were formerly so fearful and confused were completely transformed. They were "reborn" through the action of the Holy Spirit.

What a wonderful and powerful story. How unfortunate that for so many it remains just that—a nice story with no real effect in their personal lives. So many have missed the real point of the story: The promise of the Holy Spirit was not just for the Apostles. The Holy Spirit was meant personally for each and every one of us. We find this fact confirmed by several stories in the Acts of the Apostles, *(cf. Acts 8:14-24; 19:1-7; 10:44-48; 11:15-17)* but most notably in the conversion and baptism of the Gentile Cornelius.

Luke apparently considered this story so important that he told it not once but twice. The story is related as it happened in Acts 10 and then repeated in Acts 11, as Luke reports Peter's explanation of the event to the Church at Jerusalem. Peter says explicitly that "the holy Spirit fell upon them as it had upon us at the beginning" *(Acts 11:15)*.

We too have received the Holy Spirit through the sacraments of baptism and confirmation, but for many it does not seem to be quite the same as what Luke describes in the Acts of the Apostles. And yet we know that it is the same because there is only one Holy Spirit. Perhaps, if we do not experience the fullness of the Holy Spirit as the Apostles did, it is because we have not followed their example of prayer. In his second letter to Timothy, Paul says, "I remind you to stir into flame the gift of God that you have through the imposition of my hands" *(2 Tim 1:6)*. Perhaps we too should follow that advice as we continually ask for the gift of the Holy Spirit.

PRAYER: Lord Jesus, send forth Your Spirit as at a new Pentecost. Fill us, Lord, with Your Holy Spirit, that we too, might be Your witnesses, to the ends of the earth.

The Fourth Glorious Mystery

The Assumption

REFLECTION: Jesus has promised us all a share in the glory of the Resurrection. We will be Resurrected from the dead one day and be given a glorified body. The Last Judgment and the bodily Resurrection will constitute the final chapter and the completion of our redemption, which has been gained through the merits and sacrifice of our Redeemer, Jesus Christ.

Mary, who was born without sin, who lived without sin and who always responded to God's grace with faith and humility, has already received the fulfillment of that promise. When her life on earth was completed, she who gave birth to the Redeemer and always lived in the light of redemption, was taken up into Heaven, her glorified body united with her immaculate soul. Once more Mother and Son were together, never more to be separated. Such has been the constant belief of the Church, as recorded in many early writings and definitively declared by Pope Pius XII in 1950.

Saint Paul tells us that "eye has not seen, and ear has not heard" *(1 Cor 2:9)* the wonders God has prepared. We look forward with great hope and anticipation to that glorious day when we join Jesus and Mary in the fulfillment of that promise.

PRAYER: Mary, Mother of God and our own mother, pray for us, intercede for us and obtain for us the grace to understand the depth of the promise, so that we might be encouraged to draw ever closer to your Son Jesus. Help us turn our backs to sin and Satan, that we might learn to respond as you did Mary, with faith and humility.

The Fifth Glorious Mystery

The Crowning of Mary as Queen of Heaven

REFLECTION: Jesus Christ, true God and true man, is Lord of all the universe; He has dominion over all that is seen and unseen and His rule is everlasting. He has rightly been called the King of Kings. It is only natural that the mother of the King should be given the title of Queen. Mary, who was humble and hidden in her earthly life, has been exalted above all creatures in the next.

Some have complained that we may decrease devotion to Jesus by giving Mary such an exalted position, that they compete for our allegiance. Rest assured, there is no competition in Heaven. It is we who sometimes manufacture competition in failing to realize that the will of Mary conforms totally to the will of God.

It was God who saw fit to exalt Mary when He sent the Angel Gabriel to ask her cooperation in His divine plan of redemption. Our Heavenly Father proclaimed her *highly favored* and *blessed among women* and we are only following His example when we honor Mary. What Jesus has by His very nature, Mary has through the grace of God. Jesus seeks only to give us eternal life and bring us into the Kingdom; Mary seeks only to bring us unto her Son, just as she was pleased to bring Him unto the world.

The recognition of Mary as Queen of Heaven can be traced back to early times. Scripture provides little direct evidence of Mary's Queenship, but in Chapter 12 of the Book of Revelation, John describes his vision: "A great sign appeared in the sky, a women clothed with the sun, with the moon under her feet, and on her head a crown of twelve stars" *(Rev 12:1)*. Some have seen in the *woman*, Mary, the Queen of Heaven, while many others have seen an image of Israel; both the old Israel that brought forth the Messiah as well as the New Israel, the Church, that continues to bring Christ into the world. Perhaps both views can be considered correct if we follow Saint Bonaventure's thoughts that the woman is literally Mary and mystically the Church. This view seems in harmony with the current emphasis on Mary as model of the Church; a teaching expounded as early as the fourth century by Saint Ambrose and confirmed as recently as the Second Vatican Council.

Many early writers, including St. Ephraem, St. Gregory Nazianzen, St. Jerome, St. Peter Chrysologus, and St. John Damascene have referred to Mary as Queen. In the Cathedral of Parenzo located on the Adriatic about halfway between Triest, Italy and Pula, Croatia there is a mosaic of Mary, Queen of Heaven, which dates back to the year 540. As we meditate and ponder Mary's Queenship, let us rejoice and thank God that our Queen is also our mother and that her only desire is to conduct her children into the presence of the King, so that we might have life everlasting.

PRAYER: Mary, Queen of Heaven and Queen of our lives, guide us on our journey through life. Show us the way to your Son, bring Him into our hearts and teach us to love Him as you have loved Him.

A Final Note

Legend has it that Our Lady told Saint Dominic that one day she would save the world through the Rosary. Although the historical accuracy of that legend is questionable, the message certainly does have value. The Rosary, with its meditations on our Lord and His mother, is a valuable aid to spiritual awareness and development. It has been recommended by many popes and saints throughout the ages. Our own U.S. Bishops have also recommended the Rosary in their November 21, 1973 pastoral letter entitled *Behold Your Mother, Woman of Faith*. Let us resolve to say the Rosary not only in October but every day of the year.

XVIII

November

The Month of Holy Souls

The Christian tradition of praying for the deceased goes back to the time of the Apostles and there is a Jewish tradition of praying for the dead which predates the Christian tradition *(cf. 2 Maccabees 12:46)*. November has long been a special time to remember all of our deceased loved ones.

The month begins with the feast of All Saints. Throughout the year, certain days are designated to remember one or more particular canonized saints, but on All Saints Day we commemorate *all* the members of the Church Triumphant whether canonized or not. On that day we honor those saints whose names are known only to God and rejoice that one day this will be our feast day as well.

The following day, November 2nd, has been designated the feast of All Souls, that special day when we remember and pray for all the faithful departed who have left this life but have not yet entered the fullness of their life with the Lord. During the entire month of November, our family continues to pray for our deceased relatives and friends. As we remember those who have gone before us, we also reflect on our own final destiny. We consider the glories and promise of Heaven and briefly mention Hell, but during November our main emphasis is Purgatory.

Theologians have speculated for centuries but still they have not been able to give us a precise and certain definition of the state of Purgatory. In fact, there are only two things the Church has defined for our belief: First, we know from very early and constant tradition that such a state exists. Secondly, we believe that we, as members of the Church Militant, can by our prayers and sacrifice aid those souls on that final segment of their journey into the fullness of the Church Triumphant. In these two traditional beliefs, we find the sum total of what was confirmed and defined by the Council of Trent, but this still does not tell us very much about the state of Purgatory.

Most theologians agree that the lack of the beatific vision and loss of union with God will be Purgatory's greatest torment, but beyond that we find no general agreement. There are many other suggestions and opinions which may be helpful in understanding a mystery which we in this life can never fully comprehend.

Both Purgatory and Hell have often been portrayed as consisting of fire, but that is far from a universal view. Others speak in terms of a "purification" or rooting out of affection for sin. Many times we hear that we must *pay* for our sins and suffer the punishment of a *just* God, but it is difficult to reconcile God's justice with His mercy.

Many traditional descriptions of Heaven, Hell and Purgatory seem designed to *scare* one into *being good* rather than helping one grow as a Christian. The real Christian message is one of love, joy and hope, not gloom and despair. We do not dwell on the traditional concepts of pain and punishment in our November mealtime discussion. We generally try to take a positive approach in explaining Heaven, Hell and Purgatory, through the perspective and concept of sin as a rejection of God's plan, and the need to overcome sin as we progress toward union with God.

We begin with a discussion of Genesis 3:1-13 (see comment with Advent prayers on page 144) and make the point that we are all born into the world as selfish, self-centered people. We then go on to the rest of Chapter 3 and to the story of Cain and Abel in Chapter 4. We see in these inspired words a symbolic story of the disaster that results when man rejects God's plan. The story of Noah and the Flood further confirms the need to accept God's love and follow His plan for us.

We look at Chapter 13 of Paul's first letter to the Corinthians and see a description of love which reflects the life Jesus wants us to live, in sharp contrast to that described in Genesis. For a further understanding of God's plan as Jesus revealed it, we look at the great commandment and last judgement stories in Matthew 22:34-40 and 25:31-46.

At baptism, we are accepted into a community, the People of God, and given certain graces (sanctifying grace) with the promise of others (actual graces) to help us on our journey. Baptism does not, however, automatically transform us into loving, outgoing people. We must grow in love and begin to overcome our faults and imperfections. Jesus will offer Himself to us and will help us to the extent that we open ourselves and accept His help. His greatest desire and His whole purpose in coming into the world is to help us love one another and to show us the way to the Kingdom. He has even told us that He goes before us to prepare a place for us *(cf. Jn 14:3)*. We try to follow His way and learn to love, but there are only a few great saints who reach perfection in this life. Most of us will have to go through a purification process to atone for our sins and be transformed in conformity with the will of God.

Some theologians have theorized that we in fact will make our own Purgatory when we see ourselves as we really are. When we fully understand our own sinfulness and attachment to sin, we will not be able to bear the sight of God, who is all good. Thus, we will require that period of transformation and purification which we call Purgatory.

Anthony Wilhelm's book *Christ Among Us* (Chapters 3, 18 and 26) provides an easily understood discussion of modern theological thoughts on sin and Purgatory. *The Great Divorce* by C. S. Lewis is another book I highly recommend. Although it is completely fictional and fantasy it provides good food for thought and insight into our human nature.

Remembering the deceased in our family prayer gives the children a real feeling for the oneness of the Body of Christ, even when it spans this world and the next. I believe it has helped them develop a practical understanding of the Communion of Saints. At any time during the year when a friend or relative passes on to the next world, we offer a special commemoration with our mealtime prayers by preceding our regular blessing with the following prayer:

Eternal rest give unto him/her, O Lord,
and let perpetual light shine upon him/her.
May his/her soul and all the souls of the
faithful departed, through the mercy of
God, rest in peace. Amen.

During November, a special time to remember the deceased, we include the prayer for the faithful departed at our main meal each day. We make the specific intention to remember all our departed relatives and friends and all who have passed on to the next life. We use a slightly modified version of the same prayer, as follows:

Eternal rest give unto them, O Lord,
and let perpetual light shine upon them.
May their souls and all the souls of the faithful
departed, through the mercy of God, rest in peace. Amen.

Also during November we join together in some after-meal prayers for the departed. Some of these may be found in Appendix A4.

XIX

Thanksgiving Day

Ours is a young country whose culture and traditions have been drawn from the cultures and backgrounds of many peoples. Through the "melting pot" we have developed into a new and unique people, and yet there is very little in our culture that can be called truly and uniquely of American origin. Thanksgiving Day is a notable exception.

It was first celebrated by the Pilgrims in 1621 after their first good harvest in this country. They had suffered greatly through the previous winter, but God had blessed them through the summer; their crops were in, life was easier and they had plenty to eat. They recognized that their new-found peace and prosperity was a gift from God. They realized, as it says in the book of Deuteronomy, "when you have eaten your fill, you must bless the LORD, your God, for the good country he has given you." *(Deut 8:10)*. They had eaten well and now it was time to give thanks.

In addition to its American origin there are many unique things about Thanksgiving Day. Although it has definite religious overtones, Thanksgiving is essentially a civil holiday. It was Governor Bradford and not a religious leader who decreed the first Thanksgiving.

As our nation gained its independence and framed a new constitution guaranteeing separation of church and state, the tradition of a national day of thanksgiving continued. In his first year in office, President George Washington declared November 26, 1789 to be a day of national thanksgiving. His proclamation reflected the deep faith of our Founding Fathers, in sharp contrast to those who today would have us believe that separation of church and state means separation of a nation from its God. In his proclamation, President Washington declared, "it is the duty of all nations to acknowledge the providence of God, to obey His will, to be grateful for His benefits and implore His protection and favor." It is interesting to note that he did not say it is the duty of all people but rather of all nations, thereby implicitly including official governmental entities as well as individual citizens. He further recommended that the people devote the day to the service of God, "who is the beneficent Author of all the good that was, that is or that will be."

Another great American leader, Abraham Lincoln, further recognized our national dependence on the Almighty in his own Thanksgiving Day proclamation. In addition to giving thanks, he urged prayers in church and home to "implore the interposition of the Almighty Hand to heal the wounds of the nation and to restore it."

Recent decades have seen many changes in attitudes and values among the American people. Many no longer share in the simple faith of our forefathers; they look instead to science and technology as the giver of blessings. We're told "you've got to make it on your own" and "look out for Number One"; we've even heard that "God is dead." And yet, on at least one day of the year, most Americans do recognize the blessings they have received. It may be a true and heartfelt prayer of thanksgiving or a simple toast with lifted glass, but in one way or another, we as a nation recognize that while much of the world lives in poverty we have been singularly blessed.

Thanksgiving Day, more than any other, is a family holiday and it is the traditional gathering of the extended family around the dinner table that has made this day so memorable to so many for so long.

The joy and excitement of the day often overshadow the true meaning of Thanksgiving Day and it is well to reflect on the significance of this one day which we as a nation give back to God. Our nation has many blessings for which we should be thankful. For several years we have joined with our parish community to express our thanks for the year's blessings at a special liturgy of thanksgiving celebrated on Wednesday evening which allows us to go together as a family without interrupting the Thanksgiving Day meal preparations.

We turn also to the Word of God as we reflect on the true meaning and importance of Thanksgiving Day. Chapter 8 of the Book of Deuteronomy provides much food for thought. Although written for another people and another time, there is a certain prophetic message for us as well. A careful reading and thoughtful re-reading, paying particular attention to verses 10, 11, 17 and 19 will reveal some insight into God's plan.

The message is very simple: God has provided many blessings, but we must remember from whence those blessings come. We must turn to Him in thanksgiving and continue to faithfully serve Him. If, as a nation, we turn away from God, our days of happiness and prosperity will come to an end. Perhaps as we ponder the true meaning of Thanksgiving Day and the words of Deuteronomy we should thank Him for this national holiday which reminds us to be thankful. Let us resolve that every day we will offer thanks for the many blessings we enjoy individually and as a nation.

XX

Other Family Prayer-Learning Experiences

In the previous chapters we have spoken mainly of mealtime prayer and instruction, but spiritual development cannot be a once-a-day activity. Faith is meant to be an integral part of our everyday life and there are numerous opportunities to pass that faith on to our children. No book can ever quantify all of these opportunities, but in this chapter we will mention some that have been a part of our family life over the years.

Our family unity is strengthened each week by our attendance at Sunday liturgy. There have been weeks when we have had to go at separate times, but we make every effort to attend as a family whenever possible. The celebration of the Mass is our single most important act of worship and it is vital that our children sense its importance in their early years.

There are several ways to demonstrate this importance: The most obvious is our own faithful attendance; I think in the past twenty-five years there has been only one week when we did not participate in the Sunday liturgy, and that was because we were traveling in an area where there were no Catholic churches. On that particular Sunday we joined together as a family in the recitation of the Scriptural Rosary.

Another witness to the importance of the Mass is our attendance at daily Mass. While not an everyday occurrence, we sometimes attend Mass during the week and offer the children the opportunity to participate on a voluntary basis. It is important that they not feel coerced and know they are free to refuse. In this way, they can learn from our example that the Mass is inherently important, and not just the fulfillment of an obligation. I remember a particular Lenten season when I was going to Mass almost every day. The number of times that the whole family went were few, but even fewer were the number of times I went alone.

Another practice which seems unique to our family is our thanksgiving after Mass. This is a practice that was impressed upon me in my late teens by a priest who was a very special part of my early life. The opportunity to attend the Sacrifice of the Mass is an awesome privilege and if we really understood that privilege we would probably spend a lot more time in thanksgiving. At the end of each Mass we all kneel for a moment to thank the Lord for allowing us to be there and to have received His Body and Blood through the Eucharist.

With one notable exception, I have observed over the years that at the end of Mass most people are in a hurry to get out and yet as they crowd into the aisles there is no place to go. The one exception to this rush to fill the aisles was at a church in Minneapolis, Minnesota where at the end of Mass everyone knelt for a short prayer of thanksgiving. It seemed so unusual that I thought for sure there was more to come; perhaps benediction or prayers for a special parish intention. After a few moments, people began slowly to get up and leave. It was then that I realized they were all offering a thanksgiving for the Mass that they had just participated in. These few minutes of thanksgiving after Mass not only witnesses to our children but also allows us to become more aware of the real importance of the Mass in our own spiritual development.

Vacation trips offer a unique opportunity to demonstrate a faith which is an essential part of our day-to-day activities. Whether it be a simple day trip or a longer venture, we start with a "car rosary." We use the Scriptural Rosary and as we get under way, one of the children starts the first Mystery. Each of the children take a turn reading the Scripture verses for one of the Mysteries and we all join in for the Hail Marys. We have found this to be an ideal time for the family Rosary; there are few distractions and it is particularly appropriate as we ask our Blessed Mother and her Divine Son to guide us and protect us on our way.

Choosing places to visit can also be a witness to our faith. I recall an enjoyable family day in New York City. Everybody wanted to see the U.N., the World Trade Center and the Statue of Liberty. We saw them all and more; but we also began with morning Mass and a tour of Saint Patrick's Cathedral.

On another occasion we vacationed in Canada. Among our choice of tour sights we included the well known shrine of St. Anne de Beaupre just a few miles outside Quebec city. A fall trip to see the Adirondack foliage had as its destination the shrine of the North American Martyrs at Auriesville, N. Y.

Visits to shrines are beneficial for all ages, including younger children who particularly enjoy the outdoor Way of the Cross found at most shrines. Each reproduction provides an opportunity to explain our Lord's Passion with visual aids. Some shrines also provide reproductions of the fifteen Mysteries of the Rosary which can be used in the same way.

A one-day pilgrimage to pray for a particular blessing at a nearby shrine can also be meaningful. We made such a journey the week before the Confirmation of our three oldest children. This unique trip allowed us time to review some of the important lessons of Confirmation. We discussed the indwelling of the Holy Spirit and stressed the importance of this sacrament, through which one becomes an adult Christian. We also took the opportunity to point out the importance of prayer at the beginning of any major juncture in life.

The visiting of shrines has become an integral part of our family's spirituality. BethAnn, our youngest, often stopped at the National Shrine of Divine Mercy in Stockbridge, Massachusetts on her way home from Springfield College. And David, after working two years at Covenant House, spent a full month with backpack and sleeping bag, visiting many shrines as he walked out of Manhattan and across much of New Jersey, Pennsylvania and Maryland.

All of the places mentioned above are in the Northeast, but other parts of the country are equally blessed. In the Southwest, for example, one finds the historic Spanish missions, and in Gatlinburg, Tennessee you can find the life of Christ portrayed in life-size reproductions. No matter where you live or travel there are opportunities to include a spiritual interlude with your sightseeing. It may be a shrine in honor of Our Lady or some other saint, a monument to a pioneer priest or a church of historic importance.

Other examples include the world's largest crucifix in Indian River, Michigan and the 90-foot high statue of Our Lady of the Rockies on Interstate 15 near Butte, Montana. In St. Augustine, Florida, you find the oldest church in the United States and our nation's capitol has the National Shrine of the Immaculate Conception, which was built with contributions from all over the country.

A visit to your own diocesan cathedral can provide an opportunity to explain the unity and oneness that we find within the Church. The cathedral is the bishop's church and our unity with the bishop binds us in faith to the members of the other parishes in the diocese, thus making us one in Christ. We are further made one through our union with the Bishop of Rome. It is through that visible symbol of unity that we are reminded that we are all called to be *one* in Christ. This oneness in Christ has become even more apparent in recent years, as we observe the witness of our present Holy Father, John Paul II, and his tremendous concern for our brothers and sisters all over the world.

There are many other opportunities for parents to offer Christian witness to their children. Participation in parish activities, both social and spiritual, helps give one a sense of being a part of the People of God. Service to the less-fortunate is an ideal witness. I recently came across a quote from Mother Teresa of Calcutta: "In India there is a hunger for food. In the West there is a hunger for love. I find more poverty in the Western world—and it is harder to fight." Delivering meals to the elderly, hosting a "fresh air child" from the inner city or just taking the time to listen to someone else's problem all provide that love which the world hungers for.

We have all heard that "it is more blessed to give than to receive" and our experience has shown us that sometimes it can be more enjoyable as well. Some years ago my company sent me on a foreign assignment. We took advantage of that opportunity and traveled through several countries of Europe. Showing pictures and sharing some of these experiences with the residents of a local adult home proved to be an enjoyable family experience and was as beneficial to us as it was to those we had come to serve.

The list goes on and on, but each family must find its own unique response to God's call. That response must come from the heart, rather than a prepared list. There is no better way to pass on the faith than by example, but if one adopts a particular practice simply to set an example, it will probably fail to achieve its purpose. To be effective, Christian witness and example must come from the heart, and it is for that reason that we must first examine our own relationship with the Lord. We must be concerned with our own spiritual growth, as well as that of our children. As we begin to recognize our own shortcomings and as we grow spiritually, we will begin to set a good example for our children. If we can lead them to the realization that they must continue to grow even after they reach adulthood, we will have taught them well.

Finally, as important as it is to pray with our children, it is equally important to pray *for* them. For as long as I can remember, after each Mass, in addition to a prayer of thanksgiving, I have prayed through the intercession of our Blessed Lady for family unity and a closeness to the Lord with the following prayer:

Mary, Mother of God, pray for us, bring
us close together and close to you
and your Divine Son. Amen.

Through prayer, we have grown as a family and it is our hope that the sharing of some of our experiences will help you and your family to grow in love for each other and for our Lord, so that one day we may all gather together as one family to sing His praises eternally.

APPENDIX A1

Traditional Devotions

The choices of non-liturgical devotional exercises have varied greatly throughout the history of the Church, often reflecting the spiritual needs of the faithful in a particular time or place. Two of the most pressing spiritual needs of our time are the strengthening of Christian life and the instruction of our children in basic Christian doctrine. As we attempt to meet these needs through the family prayer-learning experience, we have attempted to draw from the rich heritage of our past.

A vast array of devotions have been passed down to us through the centuries. Some have been more widely accepted than others; over the past several centuries some have gained such widespread popularity that the Church, through the office of the Holy Father, has recommended them to all the faithful with special blessings and encouragement. Some have been designated for commemoration on a particular day, while others are associated with an entire month.

A few of the monthly devotional designations are well known and firmly established, while others are relatively unknown. In fact, for some months you will even find disagreement among the various sources of reference. The chart on the next page indicates some of the sources we have referred to and our choice for each month.

We have attempted to choose from these lists those devotions which allowed us the greatest opportunity to pass on our faith and beliefs. In most months, we have followed the most prominent of the traditional devotions, although a close look at the chart will reveal that in one month (for reasons previously explained) we departed completely from the traditional lists. The actual choice of monthly devotions is certainly less important than the need for family prayer and instruction. Each family should feel free to substitute as their unique needs and background dictate.

TRADITIONAL MONTHLY DEVOTIONS

Month	Maryknoll Catholic Dictionary	New Catholic Encyclopedia Primary List	Secondary List	St. Jude Calendar	Our Choice
January	Holy Name of Jesus	Holy Name of Jesus	Holy Childhood	Holy Child	Holy Name of Jesus
February	Passion	None Listed	None Listed	Hidden Life of Christ	Passion
March	St. Joseph	St. Joseph	Holy Family	St. Joseph	St. Joseph
April	Holy Eucharist	None Listed	None Listed	Christ Our Redeemer	Holy Eucharist
May	Mary	Mary	None Listed	Our Blessed Lady	Mary
June	Sacred Heart	Sacred Heart	None Listed	Sacred Heart	Sacred Heart
July	Precious Blood	Precious Blood	None Listed	Precious Blood	Precious Blood
August	Immaculate Heart of Mary	Immaculate Heart of Mary	None Listed	Blessed Sacrament	Immaculate Heart of Mary
September	Queen of Martyrs	Our Lady of Sorrows	None Listed	Holy Angels	Holy Spirit
October	The Rosary	The Rosary	Holy Angels	The Rosary	The Rosary
November	Holy Souls	Holy Souls	None Listed	Poor Souls	Holy Souls
December	Holy Infancy	Our Lady of the Immaculate Conception	None Listed	Advent of Christ	Advent/ Nativity

139

APPENDIX A2

Advent Prayers

The following prayers and Scripture readings have been chosen to retell the story of God's plan of salvation and provide a combined prayer-learning experience throughout the Advent season. Explanations of the readings and themes for the various weeks are interspersed with the prayers and readings to provide background information and a basis for discussion.

The head of the household or other designated family member should lead the prayers and become familiar with the entire program by reading ahead. The prayers and readings have been set down in a strict day-by-day format, but each family leader should presume complete freedom to add, subtract or modify to suit the needs and desires of the family. Spontaneity and sincerity should take precedence over formality. Each family is unique and the right program will depend upon such variables as the age of the children, past family prayer experience and cultural background.

Options have been indicated for some of the longer readings, so that an abbreviated format may be obtained by eliminating that portion enclosed in brackets [ ].

Some of our friends who have used this Advent program have reported good results from reading the comments along with the designated Scripture readings, but sometimes comments or explanations are more effective if provided in the leader's own words. You will have to decide which is best for your family, but in either case some advance preparation will be helpful. This is particularly true for the beginning of each week, when the week's theme is introduced. In the case of a family with school-aged children, it could be beneficial for both parents to read and think about the weekly theme, so they may both participate effectively as teachers in the Advent learning experience.

While the Scripture readings may be taken from the version with which the family is most comfortable, I would suggest the New American Bible to avoid confusion caused by variations in the numbering of the Psalms. Also, the New American Bible contains extensive footnotes, which can be helpful and informative.

Blessing of the Advent Wreath

The blessing of the Advent wreath may take place on the first Sunday of Advent or any convenient time before Advent. As the family gathers around the table, the leader might give a brief explanation of the Advent wreath and its symbolic significance. We begin the wreath blessing with the following prayer:

LEADER: Lord Jesus, we gather here in Your Name and we know that You are here with us because You said, "where two or three are gathered together in my name, there am I in the midst of them" *(Mt 18:20).* Let us listen to a reading from the book of Psalms. **(Read Ps 33:1-5 [6-19] 20-22)**

COMMENT: Psalm 33 begins as a hymn of praise. The Psalmist tells of God's creative powers, His plans and concerns for mankind and finally ends with the Advent themes of waiting and hope in the Lord.

LEADER: Lord, during this Advent season, let this wreath and our prayers be a constant reminder of Your saving presence.

ALL: Lord, hear our prayer.

LEADER: Lord help us to open our hearts during these next few weeks, as we prepare to celebrate the birth of our Savior.

ALL: Lord, hear our prayer.

LEADER: As we open our hearts, Lord, fill them with faith, hope and love.

ALL: Lord, hear our prayer.

LEADER: Lord, bless this wreath and all who gather around it during this Advent season. (The wreath may be sprinkled with holy water.)

ALL: Lord, hear our prayer in the Name of the Father, and of the Son, and of the Holy Spirit. Amen.

LEADER: We ask You, Father, that we who gather here each evening may learn to love You more and serve You better through our Lord Jesus Christ, Your Son, who lives and reigns with You in the unity of the Holy Spirit, one God, world without end.

ALL: Amen.

At this point, if the family is comfortable singing together, an appropriate hymn such as "King of Glory" might be sung.

Daily Advent Service

The format of daily prayers and readings includes the introduction of the weekly theme and responsorial prayer on Sunday (or, if more convenient, on Saturday evening) and a series of readings for each day of the following week.

On Sunday, we have a short reading, followed by the lighting of the appropriate candle(s) and the responsorial prayer, which is followed by dinner. The longer reading and explanation or discussion can be postponed until after dinner, when the children are less distracted.

After each of the daily readings, the responsorial prayer is repeated. It has also been our custom to add the traditional table grace:

Bless us, O Lord, and these Thy gifts,
which we are about to receive, from Thy bounty,
through Christ our Lord. Amen.

FIRST WEEK OF ADVENT

Theme: Creation and the Fall of Man.

In the first week of Advent, we begin by recalling that God is the Creator of all things and the Author of all life; then we examine man's rejection of God's plan. The daily readings and responsorial prayer have been chosen to help us call to mind our own sinful nature.

First Sunday

The first reading is rather long and it might be better if the latter portions were briefly summarized by the leader. The brackets [ ] indicate good breaking points. It could also be read and discussed the night before, with verses 1-5 repeated on Sunday.

LEADER: Read Genesis 1:1-3

FAMILY MEMBER: Light one purple candle. (This first lighting will be more dramatic and symbolic if the room is dark or dimly lit.)

LEADER: Read Genesis 1:4-5, [6-13], [14-27], [28-31], [2:1-4]

ALL: Lord God, we praise You and thank You for all of creation. Bless us, O Lord, and these Thy gifts, which we are about to receive from Thy bounty through Christ our Lord. Amen.

COMMENT: In this reading we quickly discover the principle theme that God created all things, but there is another idea which should also be considered: As you read through the first chapter of Genesis observe the number of times you encounter the phrase, "God saw how good it was." As we ponder the repetition of that phrase, we realize that God made all things good and it is only their misuse which detracts from the wonder of God's creation.

LEADER: Read (after dinner) Genesis 3:1-13. The candle should be extinguished with verse 7, to symbolize that sin blocks the light of salvation.

ALL: Lord Jesus, help us to look into our hearts and find our own faults and selfishness.

COMMENT: Chapter 3 is the story of the fall of man. A verse-by-verse examination provides us with valuable insight into our own human nature and thoughts for serious reflection. Verse 1 reminds us that Satan (traditionally considered to be a fallen angel) is intelligent and cunning. Certainly we can substantiate that thought when we consider the times we have encountered attractive temptations. We find also that the serpent poses a question and attempts to bring about confusion and doubt. Have we not also experienced questioning thoughts when we considered moral decisions?

In verses 2 and 3 we find that God had a plan for the man and woman and she knew what God's plan was. She also knew the consequences of substituting a human plan for God's plan. God has formed each of us as a creature of His love and has formulated a plan for us that will assure our happiness in both this life and the next. God has made His plan known to us first through the prophets and then through His own Son, who became one of us to show us the way, the truth and the life. We were given the Ten Commandments, which Jesus summarized in two commandments: Love God with your whole heart and mind, and love your neighbor as yourself. In the Gospel of John we find that in His final days with the Apostles, Jesus gave us His great commandment: "love one another as I love you" (Jn 15:12). Finally, we have been given the Church to help us interpret and understand God's plan for us; all we have to do is follow that plan and we will have happiness and life everlasting.

Perhaps we should also note that a comparison of Genesis 3:3 with Genesis 2:17 indicates that the woman has inserted the additional prohibition of touch into God's command. We too sometimes err when we interpret God's laws with more strictness than He intended.

In verse 4 the serpent continues to sow doubt and questions the seriousness of the punishment. Verse 5 appeals to human pride and reminds us of how we always want to be master of our own destiny; we want to be "in charge" and decide right and wrong for ourselves, in accordance with our own self-interest.

The woman considers the temptation in verse 6 in much the same way that we look at temptation. There is generally some appearance of good in each temptation, something desirable and apparently beneficial. It is on this apparent good that we often focus our attention, and then we succumb as the woman did; "and she also gave some to her husband" *(Gen 3:6)*. How often have we, in our attempts to convince ourselves, tried to include someone else in our sin? Human nature does not like to be isolated in guilt and iniquity. Her husband succumbed to the temptation with no resistance, thereby demonstrating the weakness of our human nature when confronted by someone close to us.

Verses 7-13 show us some of the immediate results of sin. Who has not experienced the feeling of mental nakedness and vulnerability that often accompanies guilt? How often our attempts to avoid detection actually call attention to us and give us away. We even begin our own punishment, as we brood inside and try to avoid detection.

When the man's fault is discovered he does what we often do—he tries to put the blame onto someone else. He even blames God when he says, "The woman whom you put here" *(Gen 3:12)*. The woman, too, tries to "pass the buck" when she says, "The serpent tricked me" *(Gen 3:13)*.

As we re-read the first 13 verses of Chapter 3 with this new insight, it becomes apparent that sin entered the world as a result of pride, selfishness and the desire to plan one's own destiny, without regard to God's plan for happiness.

What a contrast between the pride and selfishness of this story and the story of love and service presented to us by Jesus. As we ponder God's plan for us and the commandment of Jesus to love one another we might look to Paul's first letter to the Corinthians for a definition of love. We should read that definition *(1 Cor 13:4-7)* through once as it is written and then go back and re-read it, substituting the word "Jesus" for the word love. A third (slow and thoughtful) reading substituting our own names for the word love can give us personal insight and understanding as we begin our Advent preparations for our Savior's coming on Christmas.

First Monday

LEADER: Read Wisdom [2:1-5], 2:6-9, [10-20], 21-24.

ALL: Lord Jesus, help us to look into our hearts and find our own faults and selfishness.

FAMILY MEMBER: Light one purple candle. (We light the candle after the reading and responsorial prayer to represent the light of Christ in response to our prayer.)

ALL: Bless us, O Lord, and these Thy gifts, which we are about to receive, from Thy bounty, through Christ our Lord. Amen.

COMMENT: This reading sets forth an erroneous philosophy of life and ends with a brief summary of man's creation and fall, as discussed on the previous day.

First Tuesday

LEADER: Read Mark 7:21-23.

ALL: Lord Jesus, help us to look into our hearts and find our own faults and selfishness.

FAMILY MEMBER: Light one purple candle.

ALL: Bless us, O Lord, and these Thy gifts, which we are about to receive, from Thy bounty, through Christ our Lord. Amen.

COMMENT: Our Lord provides a list of sins to be avoided.

First Wednesday

LEADER: Read Psalm 14:1-4a, [4b-6], 7.

ALL: Lord Jesus, help us to look into our hearts and find our own faults and selfishness.

FAMILY MEMBER: Light one purple candle.

ALL: Bless us, O Lord, and these Thy gifts, which we are about to receive, from Thy bounty, through Christ our Lord. Amen.

COMMENT: The Psalmist tells of corruption and ends with a prayer for salvation.

First Thursday

LEADER: Read Psalm 36:2-10.

ALL: Lord Jesus, help us to look into our hearts and find our own faults and selfishness.

FAMILY MEMBER: Light one purple candle.

ALL: Bless us, O Lord, and these Thy gifts, which we are about to receive, from Thy bounty, through Christ our Lord. Amen.

COMMENT: This Psalm begins with a warning that sin can take over a person's thoughts, thereby leading to more sin (verses 2-5) and continues with praise for God's protection (verses 6-10).

First Friday

LEADER: Read Psalm 52:3-11.

ALL: Lord Jesus, help us to look into our hearts and find our own faults and selfishness.

FAMILY MEMBER: Light one purple candle.

ALL: Bless us, O Lord, and these Thy gifts, which we are about to receive, from Thy bounty, through Christ our Lord. Amen.

COMMENT: Psalm 52 tells of evil and corruption which brings on God's punishment and ends with words of thanks and praise.

First Saturday

LEADER: Read Psalm 51:1-10, [11-14], [17-20].

ALL: Lord Jesus, help us to look into our hearts and find our own faults and selfishness.

FAMILY MEMBER: Light one purple candle.

ALL: Bless us, O Lord, and these Thy gifts, which we are about to receive, from Thy bounty, through Christ our Lord. Amen.

COMMENT: This is a plea for mercy, forgiveness and salvation.

SECOND WEEK OF ADVENT

Theme: God's promise of salvation.

Having spent the preceding week examining our conscience and becoming aware of our sins, we should be ready to look for the promise of salvation. During this week we will look at some of the early prophecies and the promise to King David. This week we will find in Sacred Scripture the hope and expectation of salvation which we will find in even greater detail next week.

Second Sunday

LEADER: Read Genesis 3:15 and Genesis 12:1-3.

ALL: Lord Jesus, show us the light of Your salvation.

FAMILY MEMBER: Light two purple candles.

ALL: Bless us, O Lord, and these Thy gifts, which we are about to receive, from Thy bounty, through Christ our Lord. Amen.

COMMENT: Genesis 3:15 is the first recorded instance of the promise of salvation. Genesis 12:1-3 is the promise given to Abram (who became Abraham), the father of the Jewish Nation.

LEADER: Read (after dinner) 2 Samuel 7:1-17.

COMMENT: In this reading, we find the promise and the basis for the expectation of a Messiah who will be a descendant of King David. It was customary in the time of the Jewish Kings for the royal household to include one or more prophetic advisors. One such advisor to King David was the prophet Nathan, and it was through Nathan that God revealed His message and promise to David. This promise was a central theme in the Jewish Messianic expectations and is repeated directly and indirectly throughout the prophetic books and the Psalms.

   During this week, we will look at some of these references and begin to see the unfolding and development of God's plan for salvation.

Second Monday

LEADER: Read Psalm 63:1-5, 9, [Psalm 85:1-9], [10-14].

ALL: Lord Jesus, show us the light of Your salvation.

FAMILY MEMBER: Light two purple candles.

ALL: Bless us, O Lord, and these Thy gifts, which we are about to receive, from Thy bounty, through Christ our Lord. Amen.

COMMENT: The theme of today's readings is a longing for God and a desire for salvation. While these Psalms are not specifically Messianic in nature, they do recall the attitude of longing for the fulfillment of God's promise.

Second Tuesday

LEADER: Read Psalm 89:1-5 [20-38].

ALL: Lord Jesus, show us the light of Your salvation.

FAMILY MEMBER: Light two purple candles.

ALL: Bless us, O Lord, and these Thy gifts, which we are about to receive, from Thy bounty, through Christ our Lord. Amen.

COMMENT: Psalm 89 is one of the principle repetitions of God's promise to David through the prophet Nathan.

Second Wednesday

LEADER: Read Psalm 132: [1-10], 11-13, [14-18].

ALL: Lord Jesus, show us the light of Your salvation.

FAMILY MEMBER: Light two purple candles.

ALL: Bless us, O Lord, and these Thy gifts, which we are about to receive, from Thy bounty, through Christ our Lord. Amen.

COMMENT: Psalm 132 also recalls God's promise to David. We should begin to see the central place of that promise during the centuries of waiting and preparation for the fulfillment in Jesus Christ.

Second Thursday

LEADER: Read Ezekiel 37: [15-22], 23-28.

ALL: Lord Jesus, show us the light of Your salvation.

FAMILY MEMBER: Light two purple candles.

ALL: Bless us, O Lord, and these Thy gifts, which we are about to receive, from Thy bounty, through Christ our Lord. Amen.

COMMENT: Written hundreds of years after King David, the references to David in this reading would seem to refer to the promised Messiah. Although this passage is somewhat obscure, in light of what we know of the Messiah and the New Covenant, it is unmistakably a Messianic prophecy.

Second Friday

LEADER: Read Jeremiah 30:8-9, Hosea 3:5.

ALL: Lord Jesus, show us the light of Your salvation.

FAMILY MEMBER: Light two purple candles.

ALL: Bless us, O Lord, and these Thy gifts, which we are about to receive, from Thy bounty, through Christ our Lord. Amen.

COMMENT: Another vague reference to a future Messianic time. Again, the Messiah is called David.

Second Saturday

LEADER: Read Isaiah 61:1-3 [Luke 4:14-21].

ALL: Lord Jesus, show us the light of Your salvation.

FAMILY MEMBER: Light two purple candles.

ALL: Bless us, O Lord, and these Thy gifts, which we are about to receive, from Thy bounty, through Christ our Lord. Amen.

COMMENT: This passage from Isaiah was read by Jesus, and He proclaimed its fulfillment in Himself *(cf. Lk 4:14-21).*

THIRD WEEK OF ADVENT

Theme: The promise grows stronger and clearer.

As we come closer to Christmas we will look at some of the prophecies that specifically and unmistakably refer to Jesus Christ.

Third Sunday

LEADER: Read Isaiah 12:1-6.

ALL: Lord Jesus, prepare our hearts to receive Your peace and salvation.

FAMILY MEMBER: Light two purple candles and one rose-colored candle.

ALL: Bless us, O Lord, and these Thy gifts, which we are about to receive, from Thy bounty, through Christ our Lord. Amen.

COMMENT: This song of praise written in the future tense recalls the expectation of Messianic times.

LEADER: Read (after dinner) Isaiah 11:1-10.

COMMENT: Although some of Chapter 11 is written in symbolic language, it unmistakably refers to the Messiah and Messianic times. Jesse was King David's father; the reference in verses 1 and 10 recall again the promise that the Messiah will be a descendant of David. Verses 2 and 3 give us the traditional list of the gifts of the Holy Spirit found in abundance in the Messiah and in which we now have a share as members of Christ's Mystical Body. The symbolic descriptions of peace on Earth may seem unwarranted in light of the war and strife that we still witness in the world today, but for those who have come to know Jesus in their hearts, there is no mistaking the peace and joy that He brings. That peace and joy cannot be adequately described in mere words, so perhaps it is best described in symbolic terms. We note also in verse 10 the reference to the Gentiles, and rejoice that the salvation we await is not for the Jews alone. It is to be offered first to the Jews and then extended to the Gentiles, who are destined to become the *New Israel* in the New Covenant.

Third Monday

LEADER: Read Jeremiah 31:31-34.

ALL: Lord Jesus, prepare our hearts to receive Your peace and salvation.

FAMILY MEMBER: Light three candles (two purple, one rose-colored).

ALL: Bless us, O Lord, and these Thy gifts, which we are about to receive, from Thy bounty, through Christ our Lord. Amen.

COMMENT: This reading contains the promise of the New Covenant that Jesus established at the Last Supper and on the Cross.

Third Tuesday

LEADER: Read Isaiah 42:1-4 [5-7].

ALL: Lord Jesus, prepare our hearts to receive Your peace and salvation.

FAMILY MEMBER: Light three candles (two purple, one rose-colored).

ALL: Bless us, O Lord, and these Thy gifts, which we are about to receive, from Thy bounty, through Christ our Lord. Amen.

COMMENT: This is the first of four *Servant Songs* that tell us in only slightly obscure language what to expect in the Messiah. These oracles *(Is 42:1-7; 49:1-7; 50:4-11; 52:13-53:12)* so well understood by Jesus *(cf. Lk 9:22, 44; Mk 9:12, 31; Mt 16:21; 17:22; Jn 12:32)* were apparently misunderstood by His contemporaries, who expected a powerful earthly king, rather than a "suffering servant."

Third Wednesday

LEADER: Read Isaiah [52:13–53:3], 53:4-7, [8-12].

ALL: Lord Jesus, prepare our hearts to receive Your peace and salvation.

FAMILY MEMBER: Light three candles (two purple, one rose-colored).

ALL: Bless us, O Lord, and these Thy gifts, which we are about to receive, from Thy bounty, through Christ our Lord. Amen.

COMMENT: This, the fourth of the *Servant Songs,* gives us a vivid description of the Passion of our Lord written some 700 years before His birth. This prophecy clearly tells us He has (willingly) suffered for our sins and paid the price for our offenses.

Third Thursday

LEADER: Read Micah 5:1, 3-4a.

ALL: Lord Jesus, prepare our hearts to receive Your peace and salvation.

FAMILY MEMBER: Light three candles (two purple, one rose-colored).

ALL: Bless us, O Lord, and these Thy gifts, which we are about to receive, from Thy bounty, through Christ our Lord. Amen.

COMMENT: Not only do the prophets tell us of His times and His sufferings, they actually tell us the place of His birth hundreds of years before its fulfillment.

Third Friday

LEADER: Read Isaiah 7:14; 9:5-6.

ALL: Lord Jesus, prepare our hearts to receive Your peace and salvation.

FAMILY MEMBER: Light three candles (two purple, one rose-colored).

ALL: Bless us, O Lord, and these Thy gifts, which we are about to receive, from Thy bounty, through Christ our Lord. Amen.

COMMENT: In this passage *(Is 7:14)*, the prophet Isaiah tells us the Messiah is to be born of a virgin and His Name will be *God with us.* In Chapter 9, we find further reference to His Name. As we read verse 5 we should understand that in this context, to name someone is to tell who and what he is and describe his characteristics.

Third Saturday

LEADER: Read Daniel [7:1-12], 7:13-14.

ALL: Lord Jesus, prepare our hearts to receive Your peace and salvation.

FAMILY MEMBER: Light three candles (two purple, one rose-colored).

ALL: Bless us, O Lord, and these Thy gifts, which we are about to receive, from Thy bounty, through Christ our Lord. Amen.

COMMENT: A review of the Gospels will show that Jesus overwhelmingly preferred the title "Son of Man." This title, which we find in Daniel's vision, is unquestionably Messianic and was further amplified in some of the Jewish apocryphal literature, in particular the book of Enoch.

FOURTH WEEK OF ADVENT

Theme: Prepare the way of the Lord.

The promise has been made, expectations are high, and now we see events unfold as we approach the Christmas holiday. The number of days in this fourth week will vary from one to seven, depending on which day of the week Christmas occurs. The daily readings have been chosen with the assumption of a full week. If there are less than seven days, the leader must decide how many of the week-day readings will be included, and on what days. As an aid in this task, I have placed a number in parentheses next to each of the daily designations, to indicate a suggested importance, with #1 being most important and #6 being the first choice for elimination.

Fourth Sunday

LEADER: Read Isaiah 40:[1-2], 3-5.

ALL: Lord Jesus, as we approach this Christmas season, come into our hearts and remain with us always.

FAMILY MEMBER: Light four candles.

ALL: Bless us, O Lord, and these Thy gifts, which we are about to receive, from Thy bounty, through Christ our Lord. Amen.

COMMENT: Just as Israel's service and exile came to an end, so too our Advent preparations are coming to an end as we draw close to Christmas.

LEADER: Read (after dinner) John 1:19-34.

COMMENT: Although this event takes place almost thirty years after the birth of Jesus, it is a traditional Advent story as we look forward not only to the birth of the Savior but to His mission of salvation as well. The words of Isaiah, written some 700 years before, become the rallying cry of John the Baptist as he prepares for the advent of the public ministry of Jesus. John is the precursor of Jesus, of whom Scripture says:

> "Behold, I am sending my messenger ahead of you,
> he will prepare your way before you"
> (Lk 7:27; cf. Malachi 3:1).

The one of whom Jesus said, "I tell you, among those born of women, no one is greater than John; yet the least in the kingdom of God is greater than he." (Lk 7:28).

Fourth Monday (6)

LEADER: Read Matthew 3:1-12.

ALL: Lord Jesus, as we approach this Christmas season,

come into our hearts and remain with us always.

FAMILY MEMBER: Light four candles.

ALL: Bless us, O Lord, and these Thy gifts, which we are about to receive, from Thy bounty, through Christ our Lord. Amen.

COMMENT: All the Gospel writers tell the story of John the Baptist. John was a well-know prophet who proclaimed the imminent coming of the Lord.

Fourth Tuesday (5)

LEADER: Read Psalm 47:1-10.

ALL: Lord Jesus, as we approach this Christmas season, come into our hearts and remain with us always.

FAMILY MEMBER: Light four candles.

ALL: Bless us, O Lord, and these Thy gifts, which we are about to receive, from Thy bounty, through Christ our Lord. Amen.

COMMENT: This Psalm tells of the universal Kingship of the Messiah.

Fourth Wednesday (3)

LEADER: Read Psalm 110:1-4.

ALL: Lord Jesus, as we approach this Christmas season, come into our hearts and remain with us always.

FAMILY MEMBER: Light four candles.

ALL: Bless us, O Lord, and these Thy gifts, which we are about to receive, from Thy bounty, through Christ our Lord. Amen.

COMMENT: This is an important Messianic Psalm, which

Jesus refers to in Matthew 22:41-46. See also Acts 2:34; 1 Cor 15:25; Heb. 1:13.

Fourth Thursday (4)

LEADER: Read Psalm 72:1-11.

ALL: Lord Jesus, as we approach this Christmas season, come into our hearts and remain with us always.

FAMILY MEMBER: Light four candles.

ALL: Bless us, O Lord, and these Thy gifts, which we are about to receive, from Thy bounty, through Christ our Lord. Amen.

COMMENT: Psalm 72, composed perhaps as a tribute to an earthly king who was a descendant of David, finds its fulfillment only in Christ. The Messianic language indicates the hope of the people as one of David's successors becomes king.

Fourth Friday (1)

LEADER: Read Luke 1:26-38.

ALL: Lord Jesus, as we approach this Christmas season, come into our hearts and remain with us always.

FAMILY MEMBER: Light four candles.

ALL: Bless us, O Lord, and these Thy gifts, which we are about to receive, from Thy bounty, through Christ our Lord. Amen.

COMMENT: In the story of the Annunciation and the Incarnation we find the beginning of the fulfillment of God's plan of salvation.

Fourth Saturday (2)

LEADER: Read Luke 1:39-56.

ALL: Lord Jesus, as we approach this Christmas season, come into our hearts and remain with us always.

FAMILY MEMBER: Light four candles.

ALL: Bless us, O Lord, and these Thy gifts, which we are about to receive, from Thy bounty, through Christ our Lord. Amen.

COMMENT: In the Visitation, Mary provides us with an example of love and service. We also find in this reading the beautiful Magnificat, in which Mary proclaims the greatness of the Lord and her own position as humble servant.

CHRISTMAS SEASON

Theme: The birth and manifestation of Christ

Christmas is a day of great joy and celebration; unfortunately, the secular celebration has all-too-often overshadowed the day's religious significance. The extension of the Christmas celebration to include the twelve days following Christmas will help us focus on the true meaning of this blessed event.

Our family traditionally sets up the Nativity scene during the Advent season, but we leave the crib empty. On Christmas Eve we place the child in the crib, to be found there by the children on Christmas morning. When the children were younger, we would have them gather round the crib and sing "Happy Birthday" to Jesus in order to recall whose birthday we celebrate. Only after the visit to the crib would we begin to open our own presents.

On Christmas Day, a single white candle is placed in the center of the Advent wreath. When lit, this candle represents Christ as the one and only Light of the World. The color white represents the sinless and blameless Lamb of Salvation. A red ribbon tied at the base of the candle represents the Precious Blood which Jesus shed for our sins on Calvary. Our readings for Christmas Day and the twelve days that follow recall the birth and manifestation of Jesus as the Messiah and Savior of the World.

Christmas Day

LEADER: Read Luke 2:1-7.

FAMILY MEMBER: Light the white candle. (The white candle should be lit at the reading of verse 7, to represent the light of Christ who has come into the world. During Advent, the candles are lit in response to the responsorial prayer, symbolizing the increasing light as we pray and wait for the coming of the Lord. During the Christmas season the candle is lit at the beginning of our prayer service, to symbolize the presence of Christ, whose birth we celebrate.)

ALL: You are the Light of the World, and we thank You, Jesus, for the gift of Your light and salvation.

LEADER: Read Luke 2:8-20.

ALL: Lord Jesus, come into our hearts during this Christmas season and remain with us always. Teach us to love one another as You have loved us. Bless us, O Lord, and these Thy gifts, which we are about to receive, from Thy bounty, through Christ our Lord. Amen.

COMMENT: This is the event for which we have been waiting. We have attempted to condense and in a sense re-live several centuries of waiting and hoping during these past few weeks. We can never fully appreciate the endurance of a people who waited through centuries of expectation for their prayers to be answered. But perhaps, as we rejoice in the birth of the Savior, there is a lesson for us to learn: We should not become discouraged when our prayers seem to go unanswered. When the time is right, God will grant our requests. He who knows us better than we know ourselves will provide for all our needs.

Let us praise Him and thank Him as we celebrate the birth into the world of He who made the world.

First Day After Christmas (December 26)

FAMILY MEMBER: Light the white candle to symbolize the presence of Christ who is the Light of the World.

ALL: You are the Light of the World, and we thank You, Jesus, for the gift of Your light and salvation.

LEADER: Read Matthew 1:18-24.

ALL: Lord Jesus, come into our hearts during this Christmas season and remain with us always. Teach us to love one another as You have loved us. Bless us, O Lord, and these Thy gifts, which we are about to receive, from Thy bounty, through Christ our Lord. Amen.

COMMENT: Luke, who wrote for a Gentile audience and is always concerned with the poor and downtrodden, tells of the poverty of our Lord's birth. Luke also recalls the story of the shepherds, the poorest of the poor, and the proclamation of the Good News to them.

Matthew, on the other hand, writes for the Jewish people and is concerned with the fulfillment of their expectations. Matthew places the entire story in the context of the fulfillment of the prophecies.

Second Day After Christmas (December 27)

FAMILY MEMBER: Light the white candle.

ALL: You are the Light of the World, and we thank You, Jesus, for the gift of Your light and salvation.

LEADER: Read Matthew 2:1-12.

ALL: Lord Jesus, come into our hearts during this Christmas season and remain with us always. Teach us to love one another as You have loved us. Bless us, O Lord, and these Thy gifts, which we are about to receive, from Thy bounty, through Christ our Lord. Amen.

COMMENT: Again, we find reference to the prophets, both explicit and implicit. In the story of the Magi, we find the manifestation of Jesus to the Gentiles and an implicit reference to Psalm 72:10-11 and Isaiah 60:5-6. Matthew also shows us that the Gentiles have first received God's revelation through created things *(cf. Rom 1:19-20)* as they followed the star, but they are unable to find the full message without recourse to the Jewish Scriptures, God's inspired Word.

Third Day After Christmas (December 28)

FAMILY MEMBER: Light the white candle.

ALL: You are the Light of the World, and we thank You, Jesus, for the gift of Your light and salvation.

LEADER: Read Luke 2:21-24.

ALL: Lord Jesus, come into our hearts during this Christmas season and remain with us always. Teach us to love one another as You have loved us. Bless us, O Lord, and these Thy gifts, which we are about to receive, from Thy bounty, through Christ our Lord. Amen.

COMMENT: Jesus, who was like us in all things except sin, submits and is obedient to the Jewish law. We find also in the circumcision the shedding of the first drops of His Precious Blood.

Fourth Day After Christmas (December 29)

FAMILY MEMBER: Light the white candle.

ALL: You are the Light of the World, and we thank You, Jesus, for the gift of Your light and salvation.

LEADER: Read Luke 2:25-40.

ALL: Lord Jesus, come into our hearts during this Christmas season and remain with us always. Teach us to love one another as You have loved us. Bless us, O Lord, and these Thy gifts, which we are about to receive, from Thy bounty, through Christ our Lord. Amen.

COMMENT: The prophet and prophetess proclaim the greatness and the expectation of the Messiah found in the child, but also call to mind the sorrow and contradiction that will accompany His mission.

Fifth Day After Christmas (December 30)

FAMILY MEMBER: Light the white candle.

ALL: You are the Light of the World, and we thank You, Jesus, for the gift of Your light and salvation.

LEADER: Read Matthew 2:13-15.

ALL: Lord Jesus, come into our hearts during this Christmas season and remain with us always. Teach us to love one another as You have loved us. Bless us, O Lord, and these Thy gifts, which we are about to receive, from Thy bounty, through Christ our Lord. Amen.

COMMENT: Here we find in miniature a *type* of the contradiction of faithful acceptance and total rejection of the Messiah. Those who miss the meaning, reject the Messiah and put Him to death are prefigured by Herod. Those who are faithful to the law and prophets and understand the message are prefigured by Joseph. In both the type and the fulfillment, God triumphs, first by instructing Joseph to take the child out of danger and finally by the glorious Resurrection of Jesus.

Sixth Day After Christmas (December 31)

FAMILY MEMBER: Light the white candle.

ALL: You are the Light of the World, and we thank You, Jesus, for the gift of Your light and salvation.

LEADER: Read Matthew 2:16-18.

ALL: Lord Jesus, come into our hearts during this Christmas season and remain with us always. Teach us to love one another as You have loved us. Bless us, O Lord, and these Thy gifts, which we are about to receive, from Thy bounty, through Christ our Lord. Amen.

COMMENT: The innocent are called to suffer and die because of the sin and rejection of those who will not believe.

Seventh Day After Christmas (January 1)

FAMILY MEMBER: Light the white candle.

ALL: You are the Light of the World, and we thank You, Jesus, for the gift of Your light and salvation.

LEADER: Read Matthew 2:19-23.

ALL: Lord Jesus, come into our hearts during this Christmas season and remain with us always. Teach us to love one another as You have loved us. Bless us, O Lord, and these Thy gifts, which we are about to receive, from Thy bounty, through Christ our Lord. Amen.

COMMENT: For those who wait upon the Lord, all things will be fulfilled in due time. God's plan will always triumph. When Herod dies, God calls the faithful Joseph to return with the child and settle in Nazareth.

Eighth Day After Christmas (January 2)

FAMILY MEMBER: Light the white candle.

ALL: You are the Light of the World, and we thank You, Jesus, for the gift of Your light and salvation.

LEADER: Read Luke 2:41-52.

ALL: Lord Jesus, come into our hearts during this Christmas season and remain with us always. Teach us to love one another as You have loved us. Bless us, O Lord, and these Thy gifts, which we are about to receive, from Thy bounty, through Christ our Lord. Amen.

COMMENT: In this childhood story, Luke anticipates the greatness and wisdom Jesus will manifest in His public ministry.

Ninth Day After Christmas (January 3)

FAMILY MEMBER: Light the white candle.

ALL: You are the Light of the World, and we thank You, Jesus, for the gift of Your light and salvation.

LEADER: Read Mark 1:1-12.

ALL: Lord Jesus, come into our hearts during this Christmas season and remain with us always. Teach us to love one another as You have loved us. Bless us, O Lord, and these Thy gifts, which we are about to receive, from Thy bounty, through Christ our Lord. Amen.

COMMENT: Jesus is baptized by John the Baptist as He begins His public ministry and the manifestation of His mission of salvation. In preparation for this important event, Jesus goes into seclusion for a period of prayer and fasting. Perhaps there is a lesson here for us: We, too, should pray before major undertakings and decisions.

Tenth Day After Christmas (January 4)

FAMILY MEMBER: Light the white candle.

ALL: You are the Light of the World, and we thank You, Jesus, for the gift of Your light and salvation.

LEADER: Read John 2:1-11.

ALL: Lord Jesus, come into our hearts during this Christmas season and remain with us always. Teach us to love one another as You have loved us. Bless us, O Lord, and these Thy gifts, which we are about to receive, from Thy bounty, through Christ our Lord. Amen.

COMMENT: As Jesus begins His public ministry, He performs the first of His public miracles at the request of His mother. A more detailed treatment of this story may be found in Chapter XII.

Eleventh Day After Christmas (January 5)

FAMILY MEMBER: Light the white candle.

ALL: You are the Light of the World, and we thank You, Jesus, for the gift of Your light and salvation.

LEADER: Read Luke 4:14-21.

ALL: Lord Jesus, come into our hearts during this Christmas season and remain with us always. Teach us to love one another as You have loved us. Bless us, O Lord, and these Thy gifts, which we are about to receive, from Thy bounty, through Christ our Lord. Amen.

COMMENT: Jesus publicly proclaims the fulfillment of the 700 year old words of the prophet Isaiah and announces the advent of the Messiah. He demonstrates the fullness of His knowledge and wisdom as He correctly interprets the words of Isaiah.

Twelfth Day After Christmas (January 6)

FAMILY MEMBER: Light the white candle.

ALL: You are the Light of the World, and we thank You, Jesus, for the gift of your light and salvation.

LEADER: Read Matthew 11:2-6.

ALL: Lord Jesus, come into our hearts during this Christmas season and remain with us always. Teach us to love one another as You have loved us. Bless us, O Lord, and these Thy gifts, which we are about to receive, from Thy bounty, through Christ our Lord. Amen.

COMMENT: The response of Jesus can only be understood in the context of the prophet Isaiah *(cf. Is 26:19; 29:18; 35:5-6).* Jesus does not give a direct answer, but there is sufficient evidence for those who will accept it. The evidence is clear, but the Lord leaves room for an act of faith. For us, too, the evidence should be clear: Jesus is the Messiah, the Savior, the Lord of Heaven and Earth and yet He will not force Himself upon us; He waits for us to respond with our own act of faith.

APPENDIX A3
How to Say the Rosary

In Chapter XVII we discussed the Rosary, examined its historical development and offered some suggestions for meditation. In all of this there was a presumption of familiarity and no mention of the mechanics of how to say the Rosary. That intentional omission will be addressed in this section.

The Rosary as we know it today is a unique form of prayer that combines vocal, repetitive prayer (to teach us perseverance) with meditative prayer (to lift our hearts and minds to God). The vocal prayers are grouped into pre-defined patterns, and with each group a Mystery of our Faith is recommended for thoughtful consideration and meditation.

There are many who are faithful to the Rosary but who pay very little attention to the Mysteries. They announce the proper Mystery and then say the vocal prayers without further reference to those joyful, sorrowful and glorious happenings in the lives of our Lord and His mother. I'm sure our Lord is pleased with their diligence and devotion, and He will certainly bless them for their perseverance; but there is so much more. Each of the Mysteries provide an opportunity to place ourselves mentally in the presence of our Lord as we grow in His love.

The Rosary has been given to us as an aid to prayer and meditation, and is intended to bring us closer to God. It does that in many ways. For some, it is a daily reminder of our Lord and His mission of salvation. For others, it provides a unique lesson in humility. What can be more humbling for one who prides himself on his proficiency in prayer, for example, than to realize that God also calls him to the simple repetitive prayer of the Rosary? And what beauty there is in that repetition, as we recall the most important event in all of history. The Jewish nation waited and prepared for centuries for the coming of the Messiah. The prophets foretold His coming. Then, in the fullness of time, God fulfilled His promise. "God so loved the world that he gave his only

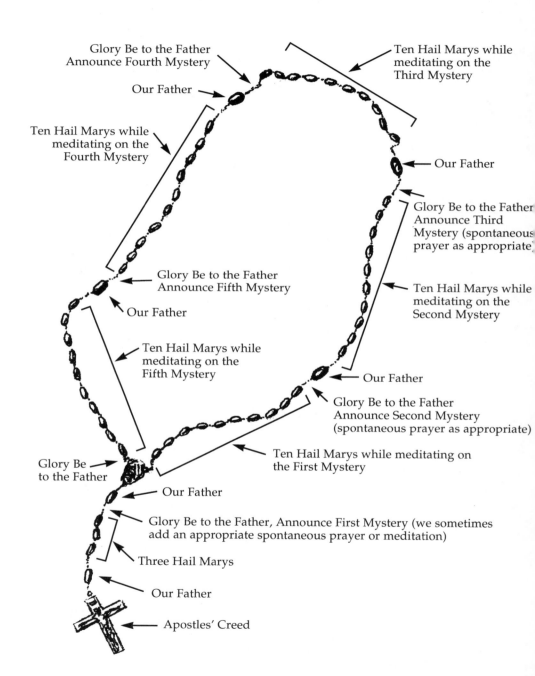

Glory Be to the Father
Announce Fourth Mystery

Ten Hail Marys while
meditating on the
Third Mystery

Our Father

Ten Hail Marys while
meditating on the
Fourth Mystery

Our Father

Glory Be to the Father
Announce Third
Mystery (spontaneous
prayer as appropriate)

Glory Be to the Father
Announce Fifth Mystery

Our Father

Ten Hail Marys while
meditating on the
Second Mystery

Ten Hail Marys while
meditating on the
Fifth Mystery

Our Father

Glory Be to the Father
Announce Second Mystery
(spontaneous prayer as appropriate)

Glory Be
to the Father

Ten Hail Marys while meditating on
the First Mystery

Our Father

Glory Be to the Father, Announce First Mystery (we sometimes
add an appropriate spontaneous prayer or meditation)

Three Hail Marys

Our Father

Apostles' Creed

Son, so that everyone who believes in him might not perish but might have eternal life" *(Jn 3:16)*. At that unique time in history, God sent the Angel Gabriel to greet Mary and announce the advent of the Messiah. It is this greeting, the Angelic Salutation, that we repeat throughout the Rosary as we recall the fulfillment of God's promise of salvation.

We begin our Rosary at the foot of the Cross and look upon our crucified Savior as we make a profession of faith:

I believe in God the Father Almighty, creator of Heaven and Earth; and in Jesus Christ, His only Son, our Lord, who was conceived by the Holy Spirit, born of the Virgin Mary, suffered under Pontius Pilate, was crucified, died and was buried. He descended into Hell; the third day He rose again from the dead. He ascended into Heaven, sits at the right hand of God, the Father Almighty. From thence He shall come to judge the living and the dead. I believe in the Holy Spirit, the Holy Catholic Church, the Communion of Saints, the forgiveness of sins, the Resurrection of the body, and life everlasting. Amen.

We follow our profession of faith with the prayer that Jesus taught us:

Our Father, who art in Heaven, hallowed be thy name. Thy Kingdom come, Thy will be done on Earth as it is in Heaven. Give us this day our daily bread, and forgive us our trespasses as we forgive those who trespass against us, and lead us not into temptation, but deliver us from evil. Amen.

We then recall the Incarnation of the Word made flesh with the same greeting the Angel Gabriel delivered to Mary at the request of God the Father:

Hail Mary, full of grace. The Lord is with thee. Blessed art thou among women, and blessed is the fruit of thy womb, Jesus. Holy Mary, Mother of God, pray for us sinners, now and at the hour of our death. Amen.

The Angelic Salutation is repeated three times and then we praise the Holy Trinity:

Glory be to the Father, and to the Son, and to the Holy Spirit; as it was in the beginning, is now, and ever shall be, world without end. Amen.

After these preliminary prayers (often offered for the intentions of the Pope) we announce the first Mystery (either Joyful, Sorrowful or Glorious). We may take just a moment to silently reflect on the Mystery and perhaps offer an appropriate spontaneous prayer. We then pray the Lord's Prayer, followed by a decade (10) of Angelic Salutations. While we continue to repeat the angel's greeting, we think about or meditate on the appropriate Mystery. At the end of the decade, we again praise the Trinity (Glory be to the Father) and announce the second Mystery. At the end of each decade, many people also add a short prayer for Divine mercy which Our Lady taught the children at Fatima:

O, my Jesus, forgive us our sins, save us from the fires of Hell and lead all souls to Heaven, especially those most in need of Thy mercy.

We continue this pattern for each of the five Mysteries. The entire process generally takes no more than fifteen minutes. The choice of Mysteries (i.e. Joyful, Sorrowful or Glorious) is optional, but generally the Joyful Mysteries are commemorated on Monday and Thursday, the Sorrowful on Tuesday and Friday, and the Glorious on Wednesday and Saturday. Many people also commemorate the Glorious Mysteries on Sundays, while others vary the Sunday Rosary according to the liturgical season.

Additional insight into the fifteen Mysteries of the Rosary may be gained through the following Scripture readings:

JOYFUL MYSTERIES *(Mondays/Thursdays/Sundays of Advent and Christmas)*

The Annunciation	(Lk 1:26-38)
The Visitation	(Lk 1:39-56)
The Nativity	(Is 7:14, 9:5-6; Micah 5:1-3; Lk 2:1-21; Mt 1:18-25, Mt 2:1-12)
The Presentation	(Lk 2:22-40)
The Finding of the Child Jesus in the Temple	(Lk 2:41-52)

SORROWFUL MYSTERIES *(Tuesdays/Fridays/Sundays of Lent)* (Is 53:1-12; Psalm 22:1-22)

The Agony in the Garden	(Mk 14:32-52; Lk 22:39-53; Jn 18:1-14)
The Scourging at the Pillar	(Mk 15:15; Lk 23:1-25; Jn 18:38–19:1)
The Crowning with Thorns	(Mt 27:27-31; Mk 15:16-20; Jn 19:2-16)
The Carrying of the Cross	(Mt 27:32; Mk 15:21-23; Lk 23:26-31; Jn 19:16-17)
The Crucifixion	(Mt 27:33-56; Mk 15:24-41; Lk 23:32-49; Jn 19:18-37)

GLORIOUS MYSTERIES *(Wednesdays/Saturdays/Sundays)*

The Resurrection	(Mt 28:1-20; Mk 16:1-20; Lk 24:1-49; Jn 20:1-31)
The Ascension	(Lk 24:50-53; Acts 1:1-11)
The Descent of the Holy Spirit	(Acts 2:1-41; Jn 16:5-14)
The Assumption The Crowning of Mary as Queen of Heaven	(Lk 1:28-30, 42-49; Rev 12:1)

APPENDIX A4

Prayers for the Faithful Departed

During the month of November, we remember in prayer the souls of our departed loved ones when we gather for the main meal of the day. We also join in some after-meal prayers for the faithful departed at some time during the month. Over the years, we have used a variety of novenas and other special prayers. One that we have used quite often is entitled *Poor Souls Novena* published by the Association of Marian Helpers in Stockbridge, Massachusetts.

We have also turned to the Scriptures for readings, and have added our own reflections and prayers. These readings, reflections, and prayers have been arranged into the following two novenas: The first, entitled **God's Eternal Word**, is taken from the Old Testament, while the second, from the New Testament, is called **Our Hope in Jesus**.

In both, the prayers are offered for the repose of the souls of our departed loved ones but the selection and arrangement are intended to give consolation and hope to those left behind in this life. Reflection on our own final destiny and God's promise can bring us comfort and peace of mind during troubled times.

GOD'S ETERNAL WORD

We have selected nine Scripture readings from the Old Testament and have added a reflection and prayer for each. We reflect on one reading each day for nine consecutive days. As the days progress, we note the constant theme of God's saving power and His preservation of the spirit He instilled within us when He created us.

Day One

The Word of God (Sirach 17:1-2, 5-8, 10)

The LORD from the earth created man,
   and in his own image he made him.
Limited days of life he gives him
   and makes him return to earth again.
He forms men's tongues and eyes and ears,
   and imparts to them an understanding heart.
With wisdom and knowledge he fills them;
   good and evil he shows them.
He looks with favor upon their hearts,
   and shows them his glorious works,
That they may describe the wonders of his deeds
   and praise his holy name.
An everlasting covenant he has made with them,
   his commandments he has revealed to them.

REFLECTION: God has created us in His image and offers us a share in His life. Heaven is our destiny and after a short time of preparation in this life we are called to join Him in the next. God is ever-faithful to His promise and His everlasting Covenant; those loved ones who have gone before us wait eagerly for the day when we will join them. Heaven is our destiny.

PRAYER: Ever mindful of Your Covenant, O Lord, we confidently ask Your mercy upon our departed loved ones, that they might enter Your Kingdom. Receive them into Your everlasting glory and lead us in this life that we might be prepared to join them when our time comes.

Eternal rest give unto them, O Lord,
and let perpetual light shine upon them.
May their souls and all the souls of the faithful
departed, through the mercy of God, rest in peace.
   Amen.

Day Two

The Word of God (Ecclesiastes 12:7)

And the dust returns to the earth as it once was,
and the life breath returns to God who gave it.

REFLECTION: The body dies and returns to the nothing from which it was made. But that is not the end of life. The soul is created for eternity and returns to God. Those who have left this life live a new life with God and one day we, too, will share in that new life.

PRAYER: Lord, You raised us up from nothing and breathed Your life into us, that we might live with You forever. In Your mercy, O Lord, grant the fulfillment of that promise to our departed loved ones and lead us through life, that one day we, too, might join them in Your presence.

> *Eternal rest give unto them, O Lord,*
> *and let perpetual light shine upon them.*
> *May their souls and all the souls of the faithful*
> *departed, through the mercy of God, rest in peace.*
> *Amen.*

Day Three

The Word of God (Psalm 49:15-16)

Like sheep they are herded into Sheol,
   where death will be their shepherd.
Straight to the grave they descend,
   where their form will waste away,
   Sheol will be their palace.
But God will redeem my life,
   will take me from the power of Sheol.

REFLECTION: When seen from this life, death is a

nether world. It seems to be an end but faith tells us it is really a beginning. After a period of purification, the departed enter into their eternal reward. It is God who redeems and guides these souls through the purification, but we who have stayed behind have an opportunity to assist them on that final journey. Our prayers and supplications speed them on their way to final union with God our Creator.

PRAYER: Purify the souls of our departed loved ones, O Lord, and lift them from the nether world into Your Kingdom. Welcome them into their eternal reward and lead us through life, that one day we, too, might receive that same reward.

> *Eternal rest give unto them, O Lord,*
> *and let perpetual light shine upon them.*
> *May their souls and all the souls of the faithful*
> *departed, through the mercy of God, rest in peace.*
> *Amen.*

Day Four

The Word of God (Psalm 116:3-9)

I was caught by the cords of death;
    the snares of Sheol had seized me;
    I felt agony and dread.
Then I called on the name of the LORD,
    "O LORD, save my life!"

Gracious is the LORD and just;
    yes, our God is merciful.
The LORD protects the simple;
    I was helpless, but God saved me.
Return, my soul, to your rest;
    The LORD has been good to you.

For my soul has been freed from death,
    my eyes from tears, my feet from stumbling.
I shall walk before the LORD
    in the land of the living.

REFLECTION: Our continued prayers relieve the sufferings of our departed loved ones. On their behalf we call upon the Name of the Lord and He saves them and gives them new life. Our God is merciful, and from His goodness He grants us eternal life.

PRAYER: Forgive their offenses, O Lord. Give them new life for all eternity and lead us on life's path, that one day we, too, might receive the gift of eternal life.

> *Eternal rest give unto them, O Lord,*
> *and let perpetual light shine upon them.*
> *May their souls and all the souls of the faithful*
> *departed, through the mercy of God, rest in peace.*
> *Amen.*

Day Five

The Word of God (Wisdom 3:1-3)

But the souls of the just are in the hand of God,
    and no torment shall touch them.
They seemed, in the view of the foolish, to be dead;
    and their passing away was thought an affliction
    and their going forth from us, utter destruction.
But they are in peace.

REFLECTION: We grieve for our loved ones who have passed into the next life. We miss them, but they have not gone far and they wait for us to join them for eternity. While we wait, we join them in prayer through the Communion of

Saints. We pray first for their salvation and they in turn remember us before the throne of God.

PRAYER: Hold them in Your hand, O Lord, and grant them that peace which can only come from You. Lead us through life's journey, that we, too, may one day join Your saints and angels in Heaven.

> *Eternal rest give unto them, O Lord,*
> *and let perpetual light shine upon them.*
> *May their souls and all the souls of the faithful*
> *departed, through the mercy of God, rest in peace.*
> *Amen.*

Day Six

The Word of God (Psalm 73:23-24)

> Yet I am always with you;
>   you take hold of my right hand.
> With your counsel you guide me,
>   and at the end receive me with honor.

REFLECTION: The Lord has created us for a greater life; He has created us to spend eternity with Him in Heaven. This life is only a preparation for our life with God in the next world and yet even now the Lord does not abandon us. He holds out His hand to guide us on our way. We have only to turn to Him and He is there. In the end, He will receive us into glory, to be reunited with those who have gone before us.

PRAYER: Receive into Your Kingdom, Lord, our departed loved ones and counsel us in this life, that one day we, too, may be received into Your glory.

> *Eternal rest give unto them, O Lord,*
> *and let perpetual light shine upon them.*

*May their souls and all the souls of the faithful
departed, through the mercy of God, rest in peace.
Amen.*

Day Seven

The Word of God (Psalm 16:9-11)

Therefore my heart is glad, my soul rejoices;
    my body also dwells secure,
For you will not abandon me to Sheol,
    nor let your faithful servant see the pit.
You will show me the path to life,
    abounding joy in your presence,
    the delights at your right hand forever.

REFLECTION: The pain of separation bites deep and the loss of a loved one can cause great anguish, but our faith tells us that one day we must all leave this world and pass into the next. We know that our separation is only temporary and that when our time comes, we will be greeted in joy by those who have gone before us.

PRAYER: We rejoice in the knowledge that our loved ones are in Your hands and that You are a merciful God. Show us Your mercy, O Lord, that one day we, too, may join them in Your presence.

*Eternal rest give unto them, O Lord,
and let perpetual light shine upon them.
May their souls and all the souls of the faithful
departed, through the mercy of God, rest in peace.
Amen.*

Day Eight

The Word of God (Psalm 121:7-8)

The LORD will guard you from all evil,
    will always guard your life.
The LORD will guard your coming and going
    both now and forever.

REFLECTION: The Lord watches over us now and forever, in this life and the next. Our departed loved ones are with Him in Heaven and one day we, too, will join them in the fullness of life which God has prepared for us since the beginning of time.

PRAYER: Lord, receive into Your Kingdom our departed loved ones and guide us on life's path, that we too may join them one day.

> *Eternal rest give unto them, O Lord,*
> *and let perpetual light shine upon them.*
> *May their souls and all the souls of the faithful*
> *departed, through the mercy of God, rest in peace.*
> *Amen.*

Day Nine

The Word of God (Psalm 23:1-6)

The LORD is my shepherd;
    there is nothing I lack.
In green pastures you let me graze;
    to safe waters you lead me;
    you restore my strength.
You guide me along the right path
    for the sake of your name.
Even when I walk through a dark valley,
    I fear no harm for you are at my side;
    your rod and staff give me courage.

You set a table before me
     as my enemies watch;
You anoint my head with oil;
     my cup overflows.
Only goodness and love will pursue me
     all the days of my life;
I will dwell in the house of the LORD
     for years to come.

REFLECTION: The Lord is indeed the Shepherd of our souls; when we walk with Him, we never walk alone. Through all manner of grief and distress, He alone can bring comfort and assure us of our hope for the future. The eternal reward which He has prepared for us is beyond our mortal comprehension. Those who have gone before us enjoy that vision and through the grace of God they continue to see us and bid us not to grieve on their behalf. They have entered into the fullness of life which God has prepared for us and one day we, too, will join them. While we wait for that glorious day, we join our departed loved ones through our prayers, which God makes known to them.

PRAYER: Lord, You have always been the Shepherd of souls; we beseech You to guide the souls of our departed loved ones into Your Kingdom and guide us in this life that one day we, too, may enter Your Kingdom for all eternity.

Eternal rest give unto them, O Lord,
and let perpetual light shine upon them.
May their souls and all the souls of the faithful
departed, through the mercy of God, rest in peace.
     Amen.

OUR HOPE IN JESUS

In this novena, we turn to the New Testament and the *Good News* message of our Lord and Savior Jesus Christ. In Jesus we find the fullness of God's plan of salvation, and our hope and joy becomes complete in the knowledge that Jesus has opened the way for us to come into the presence of our Father in Heaven. The pain and separation of death is sad, but our hope in Jesus gives us consolation and true peace and joy.

Day One

The Word of God (John 14:1-2)

Do not let your hearts be troubled. You have faith in God; have faith also in me. In my Father's house there are many dwelling places. If there were not, would I have told you that I am going to prepare a place for you?

REFLECTION: Jesus has prepared a place in the Father's house for each and every one of us. We are all special in God's eyes and He awaits each of us with love greater than we have ever known. Our departed loved ones have already entered the Father's house and one day we, too, will join them for all eternity.

PRAYER: Lord Jesus, welcome our departed loved ones into the Father's house; show them the dwelling place You have prepared. Heal our sorrowful hearts and grant us the grace to more fully understand the meaning and mystery of life in both this world and the next.

Eternal rest give unto them, O Lord,
and let perpetual light shine upon them .
May their souls and all the souls of the faithful
departed, through the mercy of God, rest in peace.
Amen.

Day Two

The Word of God (John 3:16-17)

For God so loved the world that he gave his only Son, so that everyone who believes in him might not perish but might have eternal life. For God did not send his Son into the world to condemn the world, but that the world might be saved through him.

REFLECTION: Without God, death is so final, but our faith tells us that death is not the end, only the beginning. Jesus came into the world that we might have everlasting life. Our departed loved ones have already entered that everlasting life and one day we, too, will join them in the Kingdom.

PRAYER: Lord Jesus, welcome our departed loved ones into Your Kingdom; grant them the fullness of Your promise of everlasting life. Heal our sorrowful hearts and grant us the grace to more fully understand the meaning and mystery of life in both this world and the next.

> *Eternal rest give unto them, O Lord,*
> *and let perpetual light shine upon them.*
> *May their souls and all the souls of the faithful*
> *departed, through the mercy of God, rest in peace.*
> *Amen.*

Day Three

The Word of God (John 11:23-26)

Jesus said to her, "Your brother will rise." Martha said to him, "I know he will rise, in the resurrection on the last day." Jesus told her, "I am the resurrection and the life; whoever believes in me, even if he dies, will live, and everyone who lives and believes in me will never die."

REFLECTION: Jesus has assured us of our salvation. Through the grace of God we are going to live forever. Our departed loved ones have already entered into that promise of eternal life and one day we, too, will join them in the everlasting Kingdom of Heaven.

PRAYER: Lord Jesus, welcome our departed loved ones into Your Kingdom and preserve them until that glorious day when our mortal bodies will be raised and glorified.

Heal our sorrowful hearts and grant us the grace to more fully understand the meaning and mystery of life in both this world and the next.

> *Eternal rest give unto them, O Lord,*
> *and let perpetual light shine upon them.*
> *May their souls and all the souls of the faithful*
> *departed, through the mercy of God, rest in peace.*
> *Amen.*

Day Four

The Word of God (1 Corinthians 15:20-22)

But now Christ has been raised from the dead, the first fruits of those who have fallen asleep. For since death came through a human being, the resurrection of the dead came also through a human being. For just as in Adam all die, so too in Christ shall all be brought to life.

REFLECTION: Our faith in Jesus tells us that death has been overcome. As we look at death through worldly eyes, it seems so final and yet we know that when we cross over that line we will see not death but life as it really is. Our departed loved ones see life on both sides, while we only see this side.

PRAYER: Lord Jesus, grant to our departed loved ones that fullness of life which the Father has prepared from the beginning. Heal our sorrowful hearts and grant us the grace to more fully understand the meaning and mystery of life in both this world and the next.

> *Eternal rest give unto them, O Lord,*
> *and let perpetual light shine upon them.*
> *May their souls and all the souls of the faithful*
> *departed, through the mercy of God, rest in peace.*
> *Amen.*

Day Five

The Word of God (Revelation 21:3-4)

I heard a loud voice from the throne saying, "Behold, God's dwelling is with the human race. He will dwell with them and they will be his people and God himself will always be with them [as their God]. He will wipe every tear from their eyes, and there shall be no more death or mourning, wailing or pain, [for] the old order has passed away."

REFLECTION: God came and dwelt among us, that one day we might dwell with Him for all eternity. This world will pass away but the next world will never pass away. Our departed loved ones have already been received into that everlasting world and one day we, too, will join them before the throne of God.

PRAYER: Lord Jesus, welcome our departed loved ones into the presence of the Father and let them dwell there with You for all eternity. Heal our sorrowful hearts and grant us the grace to more fully understand the meaning and mystery of life in both this world and the next.

> *Eternal rest give unto them, O Lord,*
> *and let perpetual light shine upon them.*
> *May their souls and all the souls of the faithful*
> *departed, through the mercy of God, rest in peace.*
> *Amen.*

Day Six

The Word of God (Revelation 7:9-10)

After this I had a vision of a great multitude, which no one could count, from every nation, race, people, and tongue. They stood before the throne and before the Lamb, wearing white robes and holding palm branches in their hands. They cried out in a loud voice:

"Salvation comes from our God, who is seated on the throne, and from the Lamb"

REFLECTION: Jesus is the Lamb that was slain for our salvation. He has opened the gates of Heaven and stands ready to receive our departed loved ones into the Father's Kingdom to stand before the throne of God. One day we, too, will join them in the Father's presence for all eternity.

PRAYER: Lord Jesus, open wide the gates of Heaven and grant eternal salvation to our departed loved ones. Heal our sorrowful hearts and grant us the grace to more fully understand the meaning and mystery of life in both this world and the next.

> *Eternal rest give unto them, O Lord,*
> *and let perpetual light shine upon them.*
> *May their souls and all the souls of the faithful*
> *departed, through the mercy of God, rest in peace.*
> *Amen.*

Day Seven

The Word of God (Titus 3:4-7)

> But when the kindness and generous love
>   of God our savior appeared,
> not because of any righteous deeds we had done
>   but because of his mercy,
> he saved us through the bath of rebirth
>   and renewal by the holy Spirit,
> whom he richly poured out on us
>   through Jesus Christ our savior,
> so that we might be justified by his grace
>   and become heirs in hope of eternal life.

REFLECTION: The mercy of God is without limitation. Our salvation is a free gift from a loving God. The only requirement is that we respond to His love and allow ourselves to be transformed by His grace through the action of the Holy Spirit who dwells within us.

PRAYER: Lord Jesus, show forth your mercy and grant eternal salvation to our departed loved ones. Heal our sorrowful hearts and grant us the grace to more fully understand the meaning and mystery of life in both this world and the next.

> *Eternal rest give unto them, O Lord,*
> *and let perpetual light shine upon them.*
> *May their souls and all the souls of the faithful*
> *departed, through the mercy of God, rest in peace.*
> *Amen.*

Day Eight

The Word of God (Galatians 4:6-7)

As proof that you are children, God sent the spirit of his Son into our hearts, crying out, "Abba, Father!" So you are no longer a slave but a child, and if a child then also an heir, through God.

REFLECTION: Before we were born, God knew us and made us heirs of the Kingdom. When our loved ones leave this world, it is only to receive the inheritance which has been prepared for them since the beginning of time. One day, we, too, will be called to join them in the Kingdom, to live the everlasting life God has prepared for us.

PRAYER: Lord Jesus, grant them their inheritance, which was prepared by the Father from the beginning. Heal our sorrowful hearts and grant us the grace to more fully understand the meaning and mystery of life in both this world and the next.

> *Eternal rest give unto them, O Lord,*
> *and let perpetual light shine upon them.*

May their souls and all the souls of the faithful
departed, through the mercy of God, rest in peace.
   Amen.

Day Nine

The Word of God (1 Corinthians 2:9)

"What eye has not seen, and ear has not heard,
   and what has not entered the human heart,
   what God has prepared for those who love him."

REFLECTION: Think of the most beautiful scenery you
have ever gazed upon. Think of the most pleasing sound
you have ever listened to. Think of the most enjoyable experience you have ever known. If all these happenings could
take place in the same instant, the joy and exhilaration you
would experience would still not begin to compare with
what the Father has in store for us when we enter His Everlasting Kingdom. Our departed loved ones have already
passed on to that joy and peace which the world cannot
give. One day we too will join them, and on that day we
will see God as He really is in all His glory.

PRAYER: Almighty and merciful Father, we thank You
for the gift of life in both this world and the next. We thank
You for all the graces and blessings You have bestowed
upon us. We ask that You welcome our departed loved ones
into Your presence for all eternity and that You grant us the
grace to persevere in this life, so that one day we might join
them to sing Your praises in the company of the whole heavenly host. We ask this in Jesus' Name. Amen.

Eternal rest give unto them, O Lord,
and let perpetual light shine upon them.
May their souls and all the souls of the faithful
departed, through the mercy of God, rest in peace.
   Amen.

Epilogue

In the years since Vatican II, we have seen many changes in the Church. We see evidence of the renewal which John XXIII prayed for when he said, "Let there be a new Pentecost in our day." But if that renewal is to take firm hold, it must happen within individual families.

The family must be strengthened and allowed to grow in God's love and grace; only then can the Church and society be renewed and peace be brought into the world. Each family must take up the challenge and respond to the unique plan and call that God offers in His infinite wisdom. No two responses can be exactly the same. Each family must, with God's help, make their own way, but we must also look to that larger family, God's family of mankind, and try to grow together in His love. We must share our experiences and strengthen each other.

The thoughts and experiences related in the preceding pages developed and took place over many years, as our family grew and attempted to respond to God's plan. They are offered here in the hope and prayer that other families may be encouraged and strengthened in their own walk with the Lord.

We have entered a new stage in our family life, now that the last of our children has graduated from college. I am thankful for the gift of faith that has grown within our family and it is with great joy that I reflect back on the past three decades. Words cannot adequately express the joy a parent experiences while watching that spark of faith implanted at baptism grow into a mature, adult faith. Today we see the fruits of a faith which our children now share with others.

BethAnn, our youngest, completed her masters program in special education and now serves God by serving His little ones. She was involved in a number of faith activities during her undergraduate years and spent her first postgraduate year as a lay volunteer in the Boston Archdiocese. Recently married, Beth and Art have begun their own tradition of family prayer as they join together each morning for prayer before going off to work.

Theresa rarely misses First Friday devotions and presents a continuing example of faith integrated into daily life. A strong faith developed during her teenage years has blossomed and matured; it will not be easily shaken by the cares and distractions of this secular world in which we live.

David was active in the Newman Community campus ministry during his years at Springfield College. After graduation, he gave two years of service at Covenant House, a shelter and counseling center for runaways in Manhattan. He has also worked as a full-time parish youth minister and continues to be involved in a variety of youth ministry activities. David and his wife, Carol, who was also at Covenant House for almost two years, recently established Life's Refuge Inc. as an alternative to abortion. I am confident they will continue to present a strong faith witness as they go forward together.

John, a graduate from Worcester Polytechnic Institute, has begun a career in computer programming and software development. Despite the pressures and demands of a technically oriented curriculum, he found time to further his religious education through cross-registration at Holy Cross and Assumption College, in Worcester. John brings a strong, mature faith into the business and secular world. He and his wife Debbie have witnessed to that faith as active participants in their parish RCIA (Rite of Christian Initiation of Adults) program. John has also been involved in youth ministry on a volunteer basis and was part of an advisory board for pastoral ministry to young adults in the Boston Archdiocese.

We have also witnessed that spark of faith pass on to another generation in the baptisms of Rachael and Nicholas, our first two grandchildren.

As I complete this work, I offer a prayer to God, who sanctified the family by being born into a human family, and ask His special blessings on all families. May you and your family be blessed abundantly; may you know the joy that I have known and may we all meet in Heaven one day, joining our voices with all the angels and saints to offer praise, honor and glory to the Father, the Son, and the Holy Spirit, for ever and ever.

AMEN.

August 27, 1993
Feast of Saint Monica
who, by her example, showed us the value of praying for our children